BRITISH LABOUR STRUGGLES: CONTEMPORARY PAMPHLETS 1727-1850

Advisory Editor

KENNETH E. CARPENTER

Curator, Kress Library

Graduate School of Business Administration

Harvard University

LABOUR DISPUTES IN THE MINES

Eight Pamphlets

1831-1844

Arno Press

A New York Times Company/New York 1972

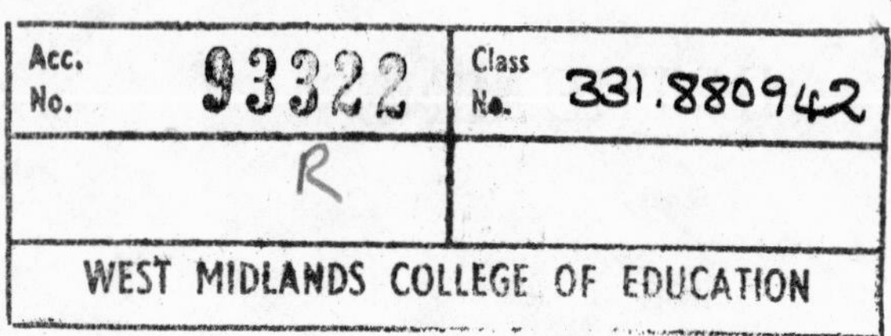
Acc. No. 93322
Class No. 331.880942
R
WEST MIDLANDS COLLEGE OF EDUCATION

Reprint Edition 1972 by Arno Press Inc.

Reprinted from copies in the Kress Library
Graduate School of Business Administration,
Harvard University

The imperfections found in this edition reflect defects in the originals which could not be eliminated.

BRITISH LABOUR STRUGGLES: CONTEMPORARY PAMPHLETS 1727-1850
ISBN for complete set: 0-405-04410-0

See last pages for complete listing.

Manufactured in the United States of America

Library of Congress Cataloging in Publication Data
Main entry under title:

Labour disputes in the mines.

(British labour struggles:
contemporary pamphlets 1727-1850)
CONTENTS: An earnest address, and urgent appeal, to the people of England, in behalf of the oppressed and suffering pitmen, of the counties of Northumberland and Durham, by W. Scott [first published 1831].--A letter on the disputes between the coal-owners & pitmen, addressed to the editor of the Tyne Mercury [first published 1832].--Report by the Committee of the coal-owners respecting the present situation of the trade [first published 1832]. [etc.]
1. Strikes and lockouts--Coal mining--Great Britain. 2. Coal-miners--Great Britain. 3. Labor disputes--Great Britain. I. Series.
HD5367.M615L3 331.89'28'22330942 72-2531
ISBN 0-405-04424-0

Contents

Also, a letter to the coal-owners of Northumberland and Durham . . . Bishopwearmouth: J. Williams [etc., etc.] 1844.

AN EARNEST ADDRESS, AND URGENT APPEAL, TO THE PEOPLE OF ENGLAND, IN BEHALF OF THE OPPRESSED AND SUFFERING PITMEN,

Of the Counties of Northumberland and Durham,

WITH A GLANCE AT

A FEW OF THE GRIEVANCES

of that Laborious and useful Body of Men;

AND HINTS AS TO THE MEANS OF

AMELIORATING THEIR CONDITION.

BY W. SCOTT.

"Rule, Britannia!..............................
"For Britons NEVER shall be Slaves." *Old Song.*

NEWCASTLE UPON TYNE:
PRINTED BY JOHN MARSHALL.
1831.
[Entered at Stationer's Hall.]

PREFACE.

For consistency's sake, it is much to be desired that the admirers of the favourite National Song or Anthem, from which we have taken our motto, would read and seriously reflect upon the subjects hinted at in the subjoined pages, before they ever again cordially unite in the festive meeting, to echo this long admired chorus.

Let us, as a people, collectively, strive to wipe the tear of sorrow from the eye of the oppressed—to ameliorate the suffering of those who are bent beneath the oppressions of the wealthy, or the perverted exercise of power or authority; and even the very effort to attain so glorious an object may give greater consistency to our enthusiasm in favour of our little "Sea girt Isle."

I here beg to state it as my opinion, that many of the Coal Owners, misled and influenced by the misrepresentations and false statements given by their Agents, as to the general situation and character of the Pitmen, remain, to the present hour, ignorant of many of their grievances; if otherwise, I conceive those grievances would no longer be allowed to exist.

Sunderland, 16th April, 1831.

AN EARNEST ADDRESS, &c.

People of England,

SELDOM, if ever, has the advocate of suffering humanity, made an appeal to you in vain, especially when that advocate pleaded the cause of the oppressed against the oppressor—of the Slave, against the relentless Tyrant who fetters and enslaves him.

To the truth of this assertion, the sable sons of Africa can bear ample testimony, that when your judgment, reason, benevolence, and humanity were appealed to on the subject of their wrongs, their oppressions, and their sufferings, that appeal was not in vain. No! all the better, the nobler, the more generous sympathies of our common nature, were instantly called into active operation; and the voice of England reiterated the cry from shore to shore, "Let the oppressed go free!" and in the servile progeny of Ham you recognized "A man and a brother."

With the African Slave, the brave people of Paris (too long taught to regard you as their common enemy) can join to testify how promptly you stepped forward to their relief and assistance, when last they made such a glorious struggle to *burst* and to *dash* in the face of their Tyrants and Oppressors, the Iron Yoke and Fetters which long, too long, had galled their Necks.

Added to these, your brave though injured, insulted, and sorely traduced fellow-subjects of Ireland will cordially unite their testimony as to the repeated instances in which you have stretched forth the succouring hand, when pale, meagre-faced famine has, like a deluge, been sweeping them from one of the most fertile spots on earth.

With these and many other such noble instances before me, it will not (I flatter myself) be in vain, that your best feelings and warmest sympathies will be addressed, when I tell you, that the cause I plead is the cause of your fellow-subjects and fellow-countrymen—yes, it is the cause of BRITISH SLAVERY to which I beg to call your attention—a slavery much more oppressive and intolerable (though it may not in some instances be so humiliating and degrading) than perhaps any regular establishment of African slaves in all the West Indies—I mean the case of thousands of your fellow-countrymen in the counties of Northumberland and Durham employed in the Coal Mines.

It is needless here to remind you, generally, that you stand more indebted to the dauntless bravery and indefatigable industry of this great body of men, for the social and domestic enjoyments of your families and your firesides, than to the exertions of any one class of the British community.

Thousands upon thousands of you, however, are totally unacquainted with the real situation of this most useful, yet most abused class of men.

You have no real idea of the dangers they every moment stand exposed to, while procuring the fuel which comforts, cheers and enlivens you round your social hearths

Equally ignorant are you of the privations and hardships to which this body of men and their families are subjected by the avaricious cruelty of their *ruthless, cold-hearted*, Egyptian Task-Masters.

Comparatively few of you know that the Pitman, before he can obtain a single particle of Coals, has to descend by a rope, from five hundred to upwards of twelve hundred feet below the surface of the earth, down a cavern, so horribly terrific and frightful, that if all the Coal Pits in Europe and the entire Continent of America, into the bargin, were offered to some of those men, who claim them as their property, on condition of their having to be looped down by a rope to the bottom of those gulphs of destruction, their dastard spirits would shudder; whilst they, with ghastly paleness, unhesitating, would reject the offer; knowing that such a descent might bring them *too near home!*

After the poor but brave Pitman descends to the bottom of this horrific cavern, he has however to walk, or rather crawl a mile, or perhaps two or three, through subterraneous vaults, where the "pestilence that walketh in darkness" hangs thick and heavy around him, and at every step he is liable to be crushed to pieces by some ponderous body from the roof; whilst the slightest inadvertency or casualty in the most distant part of the Pit, might, and often has in an instant involved him and his fellow slaves in destruction, and in many instances left the mangled fragments of his body undistinguishable from those of scores of his fellow sufferers.

But allowing him, amidst the ten thousand dangers that surround him, to reach in safety that point where his efforts and energies must all be called into action, there, perhaps, under torrents of water, equal to any incessant shower bath, he often labours from ten to fifteen hours mid-thigh deep in water; the pernicious mineral exhalations from which entail upon him a whole train of chronic diseases, and in some instances deprive him of sight, while the total absence of one breath of air fit for respiration, never fail to wear out, in a few years, the hardiest constitution. In other situations he has to extend himself at full length upon his side, and in that position, for eight, ten, or twelve hours successively, to endure and go through toil and labour that would probably kill the strongest horse in Europe—whilst the sweat falls from every pore of his body.

For the sweat thus wrung from his body, the marrow from his bones, and the blood from his veins, your humanity and generous feeling will lead you, in many instances, to conclude that the Pitman must be liberally paid and generously rewarded—but the very reverse is the case.

The poor man who breaks stones upon the high ways

is generally able to earn more money with much less labour, and without any risk of life or limb, than the Slave-driven Pitman gets for encountering all the dangers and toils inseparable from his employment.

This assertion some of you may be ready to dispute, especially those of you who have read in the Newspapers any part of the evidence given before the Committe of the House of Lords, some eighteen months, or two years since.

If we can credit Newspaper reports, (which by the bye are often vehicles of base falsehood,) there were, in the opinion of many on that occasion, statements made as base and black as ever bare-faced falsehood was clothed in. False it is thought, from those statements intentionally conveying ideas and leaving impressions on the minds of the Committee, diametrically opposite to truth.

One witness is said to have stated, upon his *Solemn Oath*, that the average wages of Pitmen was from three to five shillings per day; which average, between three and five shillings must, of course, be four shillings.—

Now all the Committee would immediately infer that Coal Hewers averaged twenty four shillings per week.

Oh! bear testimony, ye thousands of Pitmen, who seldom, the year round, have actually more than from twenty two to twenty four shillings to draw in the fortnight, after all the sharks, who are unceasingly hunting you, have made their bites and nips at the fruit of your toil and labour.

But as it is not improbable that, ere long, those witnesses may have an opportunity of explaining before the same or a similar Committee, I shall not stop further to digress in this place

But after the Pitman has toiled from eight to fourteen hours, every reasonable man would naturally expect he should get pay for all the coals he has, during that time, raised in the Pit, ready to send to bank; but no, no, this is not the case: this Slave is compelled to use a rake, and only such Coals as are too large to pass between the teeth of the rake, is he allowed to send to bank, and the remainder, (which are, in all cases, very decidedly the superior, in point of quality) he is compelled to bury in some part of the Pit, already excavated; and these are *lost*, for ever *lost* to *mankind;* a prodigal waste of what the whole human family have a common right and interest in; and for which waste generations yet unborn will execrate the name and memory of the authors of such waste.

For those small Coals thus raised, and being buried in the Pit, the poor slave who raises them is not, in many collieries, allowed a single fraction for all his toil with them; in other places he is allowed three-pence for every twenty one hundred weight so raised and buried by him, and the same if he is allowed to send any of them to bank.

The larger Coals thus raked, and sent to the bank, are subject to another sifting, and have to pass over a screen, similar to that used by masons for their lime used in building, and all the superior small Coals which falls through this screen becomes another profligate waste against society, as they are thrown up into little mountains, and either ignite of themselves, or are set fire to, and illuminate the country for many miles round, the flames of which may be seen at a distance of fifteen or twenty miles.

It is long, very long, since this scandalous outrage upon public feeling, and shameful waste of public property, has called aloud for legislative interference:—and it is to be hoped the day is not distant, when this offence against mankind will be legally restrained; an offence, by which more than one seventh part of the very best Coals in these two great maritime Counties are plundered from mankind, to gratify the stupid obstinancy and caprice, (it is generally believed) of one individual.

Thus situated, the poor Pitman's frame, in a few years, becomes exhausted, from excessive labour; and his eleven or twelve shillings a week, are found inadequate to keep soul and body together especially where he happens to have a wife and half a dozen children depending on his labour. What is to be done? why his very kind and tender-hearted employers, *(good creatures)* can better his condition by taking his dear infants into slavery, at the tender age of five or six years old.

What alternative has the poor man? to starve is rather a sickening job; and his eleven or twelve shillings a week will not feed and clothe six, eight, or ten people; of course, with a heart lacerated and agonized, he has to send his child, if a boy, at five or six years of age, to the bottom of one of those dreadful caverns.

But the period of ten or twelve hours which the older slave has to "toil at the oar," is not sufficient, in the estimation of the tender mercies of the tyrant employers, to keep the poor infant at his labour. No, no, the father is paid, (if paying it can be called) according to the quantity of coals sent to bank; but the poor young slave, being paid by the day, is required to toil away from fourteen to seventeen hours, out of every twenty four, thus leaving the infant only seven hours for sleep, refreshment, and recreation; if, indeed, it could have any list for recreation after such a period of toil in such a situation.

Oh! ye British females, let me address those of you who know what it is to be mothers—think, for a moment, what would be your feelings to be compelled to drag your infant, five or six years of age, from its bed, ere exhausted nature had half recruited her powers, or ere balmy sleep had half removed the langour and weariness of the last sixteen or seventeen hours your child had toiled—to be compelled to pull your infant from its slumbers—give it a crust of brown bread and a little milk and water, and in the very cloud of night to turn it from your door, half naked, whilst, perhaps, the lightnings glared across the heavens, the hoarse thunder roared, and the "pitiless pelting storm" descended upon its tender frame, to go to one of those yawning gulphs, at a distance of two or three miles from your residence, where it is to strive to protract its unfortunate existence by earning, in those terrific gulphs the means of purchasing another brown crust of bread !

Methinks, as it passes over your threshold, I see the tear of distracted anguish start from your eye, and the throb of frenzied madness wring your lacerated bosoms to pieces.

After having thus turned from your door the infant you had given birth to, and which you had cherished with all the doating fondness of a mother, and gazed with rapture on its infant features—your imagination would follow it to its destined den of Slavery; you would, in fancy, see it suspended by a rope, descend perhaps upwards of TWELVE HUNDRED FEET below the habitation of man, then traverse these caverns of death, a mile or two to its post, and there, like a kind of fixture, take its station in darkness, so thick and dense, that if all that infant fancy could desire were placed before it, it could not see it, or even see its own hand, till brought in contact with its little face.

Such is actually the situation of this infant for a period of fourteen or fifteen hours out of every twenty-four ; its work or employment being constantly to attend to open and shut a large door, as its other little fellow slaves drive a horse or ass past, loaded with Coals : here in patient silence it is compelled to remain, without daring to abandon its post for a moment, for fourteen successive hours—and so distant are those doors situated from each other, that the utmost exertion of its infant voice could not, in many cases, reach the ear of its nearest juvenile companion in Slavery. Thus the very eyes that nature's God has bestowed upon those children are rendered nearly useless, as they seldom open to the light of day, from Sabbath to Sabbath the whole winter round

Let English women then generally make this case their own, only in fancy for a moment, and ask themselves what would be their feelings were they the unfortunate mother of a child so situated. Yet a Pitman's wife actually has all the tender feelings of an affectionate mother, and all the sensibilities which belong to women; whilst stern fate *hitherto* has doomed her to the situation described: for should she or her family offend the Tyrants they serve, they are liable, without a moment's warning, to be drove from the cottage where they reside; and with their destitute families compelled to seek shelter, perhaps in the Parish Workhouse. For the power which the Pitman's employers hold over him, differs most materially from the power which any other British subject hold over his servants

In the Northern Counties of England there is a term made use of amongst Farmers and their servants, which has ever sounded exceeding harsh in the ears of every Philanthropist; a term at which the high-born soul of a free-born American would spurn with indignation—it is the ugly word, "Bondage Service." When the farmer engages a man and his family in his service, the work which the family do for the farmer is called "Bondage Work."

But this family, thus in "bondage" to the farmer, mightily differs from the bondage of the Pit-slave. The farmer is bound to pay his man for every day in the year, whether he can or can not furnish him with work, or whether the weather will or will not permit him to work. Not so with the Pitman. Should sickness or death in his family render it impossible for him to go to work, at any time his employers think proper to require him, not a fraction of wages is paid him for every day so absent; but should his employers, from caprice, or "any other cause," throw him idle three days in each week in the year, the Pitman cannot demand a single farthing,—but if he is so thrown idle a fourth day in ONE WEEK, he may demand, in some cases, one shilling, up to two shillings and sixpence, admitting his masters in that time find him no other kind of employment; but which work he is bound to do, however opposed to his feelings, if so required Thus is the Pitman placed in bondage much more intolerable than any other British subject, or even the West Indian slave.

But you are perhaps impatient to enquire, "What does the Pitman get for the labour of his child, of five, six, or eight years old? in which labour it has to encounter so many dangers, and endure solitary incarceration, in a dungeon more terrific than that of Daniel, or the Hebrew Children." Why, he gets the mighty sum of from eightpence to tenpence per day—admitting the little slave is fourteen full hours fixed like a statue at his post; but in no instance is there an item allowed for the time required for this infant to go to and return from its work, through the heaviest storms, to a distance in many cases of three miles from its cheerless bed to those dens of horror. No, no—blood, blood, blood, or no money, seems the favourite motto adopted by those bloated blood-suckers.

I beg it to be kept in mind that the Pitman, though thus paid by the day, is actually and positively bound and hired by the year; and if he refuses to work, under any circumstances whatsoever, he is liable to be sent, like a common felon, to the gaol, to serve his time out on the tread-mill. Then, on the Friday evening, when he fortnightly receives his twenty-two or twenty-three shillings wages, some of the viewers or overmen keep a public-house or shop, and those very trusty honest men sell various articles requisite for the poor Pitman and his family. It is true the Pitman is not compelled, by the express terms of his bond, to lay out in the overman's shop the eleven or twelve shillings a week which he receives for his toil—but we know what the fate of a brave soldier or seaman is if he chances to incur the displeasure of a vicious litigious officer: it is true also he may not that day be lashed up to the halberds or gang-way, but he may expect his fate at no very distant period. And as we know that viewers' have sharp eyes, the Pitman who passes their shops will be viewed and *reviewed*; and although the laws of our country prohibit the application of the lash to his back, yet a lash of a different kind can be applied to parts equally sensitive—to his pocket, to his belly, to his wife, and to his children;

for by a mighty authority vested in the viewers, of inflicting various kinds of fines, under a pretence of some irregularity in the poor man's work, those tyrants can, and often do, bring the poor slave into debt three or four shillings at night, after one of his most laborious and dangerous day's toil, and not one farthing allowed for all the slavery thus gone through. Oh! hear this, ye Britons, and say if any term in our language can reach the character deserved by such a system of oppression. Yet this is not a solitary case, or one of rare occurrence: no, no, it is their every day's practice. The soldier or seaman before referred to may and often does escape the vengeance aimed at him by his having to be tried by a court martial of military or naval officers, but the poor Pitman has no redress, no appeal from or against the demon who directs his poisoned virulence against him.

But perhaps you will say, "the Pitman might as well trade with his brother menial in the same employ." Yet allow it to be observed, that none of you would like to pay from tenpence to thirteenpence per pound for your candles, when you could get as good an article at the next door for sixpence, and nearly so in proportion for other articles. Yet such is the Pitman's doom.

Let it not be understood that I make those charges indiscriminately against the viewers, agents, and overmen in general. No, far from it. Many of them are men of honour, principle, and humanity; but they rarely meddle in shop affairs, but content themselves with what is considered the legal and general emoluments of their situations. But the more sharkish sort, who worm themselves into those situations, have generally a large portion of the earthworm in their composition: and it has been known that when even good and virtuous men, men of intel ect, have once incurred their displeasure, not only have they thrown that man and his family destitute, but so far has their viperous venom pursued him, as to prevent his obtaining employ wherever their interest or influence extended.

Some of you will say, "Well, but was it not stated on oath before the Committee of the House of Lords, that Coal-Owners' profits were *moderate*, very MODERATE INDEED, considering the capital sunk, and the immense risk of that capital?" I wish some of you good people of England would prevail on those who made such statements, and SWORE to the TRUTH of them, to favour you with a neat little balance sheet, containing a bird's-eye view of the capital sunk, and the different items of the disbursements and expenditure, in carrying on any half dozen collieries on the Tyne or Wear for the last thirty or forty years, each account placed distinctly separate: and against all this capital, on the same balance sheet, place in round numbers the separate income of each colliery each year, and thus silence the clamours and suspicions of the public on this subject.

Some of my readers may know, (and none more certainly can know better than some of those who appeared before the Committee of the Right Honourable House as sworn witnesses,) of a place in the county of Durham, where a knot or club of those very MODERATE MEN united some few years since, took a lease of a little place to work coals, sunk a pit, one of the most distant from the shipping port of any on the Tyne or Wear, and where those VERY MODERATE men, so situated, have, and do actually at this time, derive and reap a clear profit, after defraying every possible expence, of interest, rent, cesses, men's wages, &c. &c &c. only the VERY MODERATE NEAT CLEAR PROFIT of from seventy-four to eighty-two thousand pounds annually.

If those who know such a place, and who bore their testimony before the Committee of the Right Honourable House, would fearlessly and frankly speak out, they might thereby render unnecessary a full developement of many things which they little suspect the public are acquainted with, and which, if disclosed, must inevitably load them with, *if possible*, greater contempt than an indignant public yet hold them.

They have now an opportunity of preventing this developement; they are summoned before the great tribunal of public opinion; and this bar will, ere long, decide upon the merits or demerits of their case, not only as they have oppressed and enslaved the poor Pitman in particular, but extended their impositions and extortions to many thousands of other British subjects.

Now, if the VERY MODERATE profits arising to a band of those *very moderate men*, renting a little place as tenants, at a distance of eight, ten, or fourteen miles from the shipping port, after defraying every possible expence whatsoever, amounts to the mere fraction of from seventy-four to eighty two thousand pounds sterling yearly, upon a capital of £250,000. sunk—pray what may be the *very moderate* profit of some of those who work coals upon their own estates, at a half, a sixth, or a sixteenth part of the distance from the shipping port? I wish the Committee of the Right Honourable House would be kind enough to ask publicly the information we desire, or that the Common Council of London would take measures to obtain the information so desired, relative to the neat expenditure and income of a few of the pits for any given number of years past.

Had the Common Council of London improved some hints given to them, at the time the Duke of Wellington desired them to enquire into existing abuses in the Coal Trade, the present complaints of the Pitmen had ere now ceased to exist, and the great public inconvenience arising out of those grievances been avoided. But the Coal Owners, long skilled in political movements, managed that farce in a manner congenial to their own interests and feelings, and got only such witnesses brought forward as they approved of, and such as had an actual interest in perverting or distorting truth.

Some persons are ready to ask how far those witnesses were properly admissable (being deeply-interested parties) as competent evidence, on a question of such deep and general importance.

Yet the Committee could only decide upon the evidence given before them; but that other and more impartial evidence were not called upon is solely attributable to a culpable remissness on the part of the Common Council of London, previously appointed, by the desire of the Duke of Wellington, to investigate the subject. Those observations, no doubt, to some persons, will appear uncalled for, impertinent, and irrelevant; but I beg it to be distinctly kept in mind, that the day may not be very distant when they will appear neither foreign to the point nor unnecessary.

Thus having glanced at two or three of the grievances and calamities to which the Pitman and his family are subjected, that generous, that brave people whom I address—the people of England—are ready to ask, "Well, what can be done in the business?" —Much, very much, by a general exertion. Those brave Pitmen, no longer able to bow beneath the yoke, or to drag the chains of slavery, under which they have groaned for many years, and which yoke and chains have for the last twenty years been every year waxing heavier, and getting tighter rivetted upon them, those men in the counties of Northumberland and Durham have resolved to make one simultaneous effort to throw off their galling yoke.

You will not surely then deny to them that aid, that sympathy, that burst of indignant scorn and contempt, which you so nobly directed against the Tyrant Oppressors of the destitute, yet less injured African Slave in the West Indies, or against the execrated Bourbon dynasty of Franee. No, feeling as you do, like Englishmen, you will act like Englishmen—and again reiterate the cry, "Let the Oppressed go free!" To accomplish this glorious emancipation, a very amall but persevering effort is requisite.—Your philanthropy is constantly exhibited in favour of the children of misfortune through all the four quarters of the Globe—you cannot allow the poor untutored savage to die in ignorance, or his wretched progeny to remain ignorant of the plan of salvation—you send the *Glorious* word of life to almost earth's remotest verge—you open schools, and you liberally support those schools, where the offspring of the Heathen, of the African and of the American, are taught to read the Bible—and will you suffer the families of thousands upon thousands of your poor Countrymen to sink into worse than Heathenish darkness, which must be the inevitable consequence of the Pitmen's oppression? All attemps to cultivate the mind of a child, retorned from sixteen or seventeen sucessive hours confinement and labour, in such a situation, must prove futile and abortive, its faculties being all relaxed and paralized; and the necessary consequence must be, that this race of hardy human beings must speedily degenerate into a mere pigmy race, differing only from the Laplander in their deeper demoralization and crime.

Let then, (as a remedy against the threatened evil) a committee of management be established in everytown and village, to correspond with the parent society in Newcastle or Sunderland; let collectors be appointed, and weekly subscriptions made, according to the ability of subscribers, from a half-penny to a pound a week: and from this fund let aid and assistance be sent to the distressed families of the Pitmen on the Tyne and Wear. A very little time will this prompt and general effort be required; as the stock of Coals at present raised in this neighbourhood will soon be exhausted; therefore let the novelty be witnessed of Coals coming to Newcastle. There are plenty in Stockton, and an abundance in Scotland; therefore send away your ships to the Tees and to Scotland—and thus will you teach those despotic extortioners, who have long oppressed England byexhorbitant charges, that they can no longer outrage public feeling, fetter and cramp Commerce and Navigation, or shut up, at their arbitrary pleasure and wills, the Tyne and the Wear, by their restricted vends. Go, ye British females! your eloquence in such a cause will be irresistable—tell your generous Countrymen, and your doubly warm-hearted Countrywomen, that not only justice, honor, benevolence and humanity, all combine with *self interest;* but, above all, the sacred dictates of Christianity enjoin their most powerful sanctions and commands to enforce this work of mercy. Then tell the ship-owner, rather than moor and unrig his ship in the harbour, to send her away for coals—stimulate the merchant with this novel speculation—and while he can supply you with coals, do not order a single peck from any other place or person—at the same time get the ship-owners names, as subscribers to the oppressed Pitmen's fund.—Fear not, no mechanic, who has employment, will deny you his weekly mite to support this cause; no tradesman, no shop-keeper, no butcher, no baker will refuse you, who has it in his power to give: all will vie with each other, from a conviction that the point of the Pitman's pick is the pivot upon which rests or moves our commerce, our trade, and our prosperity.

Let me stimulate you, ye British females, not to be outdone in zeal, courage, and perseverance, by the females in France, when, in the memorable struggle in the streets in Paris, their husbands, brothers, and sons resolved to be free or perish: forgetting the natural timidity and delicacy of their sex, whilst inspired by the sacred flame of liberty! those brave and virtuous women rushed upon the point of the bayonet and the mouth of the cannon, and the dastard souls of the minions of Tyranny and corruption shrunk and fled from the contest; and the noble achievements of those valourous women, with their names, will stand recorded among the latest annals of the French nation. Your contest, (thank heaven) though of a very different complexion, is not very dissimilar in its object—the suppression of Tyranny. Go forth then, ye British Patriots, male and female, British Oppression, and British Slavery, have paramount claim upon your deepest interests and attention—remove the cause of British degradation and British thraldom, previous to extending your hand over the Atlantic Ocean. However loud and imperious the claim in favour of Africans—

yet your country, bleeding under the oppressor's lash, exhibits her lacerated bosom to your view, and in confidence exclaims, "Britons, noble, generous Britons, will no longer tolerate the infliction of those wounds and those sorrows." Go on then, and may success, fully commensurate to the JUSTICE and IMPORTANCE of the cause you plead, attend your efforts.

I would now conclude, with a few remarks to the Pitmen in general. Let me tell you, brave men, that the great object which you at present seek, becomes pretty generally known to the public, to consist simply in getting twelve hours wages for every 12 hours you labour, as no other men on earth have ever been required to toil; and the public feeling is, that the wages which you demand are so low and so moderate, that no man could be found in England, except a Coal-Owner or his Agents, who would not declare, "you ask *too little*, and are *too* moderate in your demands."—Then again you seek to obtain the little you do so earn, fully and without the felonious plunders to which you have hitherto been subjected; willing, at the same time, to submit to any fixed sum which many be settled upon, (not by the arbitrary Tyrant, to levy as his viperous venom alone may dictate,) but a settled, definite fine, for any absolute trespass against the established regulations of the trade; the amount of such fine to be settled and fixed by any number of neutral or disinterested gentlemen; an equal number of which jury, for so fixing those fines, to be one half appointed by the Owner, (*not their Agents*) and the other half to be chosen by the Coal-Hewers of each Pit.

Again you seek to lessen the period of your infants incarceration in those solitary vaults of darkness and danger, from fourteen, sixteen, or seventeen hours, to twelve hours—and you do, I believe, request an equalization of the size of the corves or baskets, which you are allowed to send to bank—and you complain of only getting pay for twenty corves so worked, when you have in all cases to send twenty one or twenty two corves to bank. You further beg to be placed in such circumstances that your oppressors may not, without one moment's notice, have it in their power to throw you and your destitute family to the streets, at the capricious impulse of their own will. These, with a few minor points I presume, include the principal grievances: yet be it remembered, that I make those statements, not from any regular meeting, either of your Committee or Delegates. But I beg my reader to turn over the last two or three pages of this address—then he must not breathe the sentiments or feelings of an Englishman who will name any one demand made by the Pitmen as exhorbitant, unjust, or extravagant.

It is not yet out of the recollection of many, that when coals were sold for twelve or fourteen shillings per chaldron, that Pitmen at that time got more than double the money they now do; and yet Coal-Owners were then *very seldom* sent to Gaol, although quite unacquainted with the mechanical powers which now afford them so many advantages and facilities in working Coal; but this great field is far too extensive and wide to even glance at here.

Let me tell you then, brave Pitmen, that the general steadiness of your conduct and deportment, the very unexampled patience and forbearance you have already exhibited, has got you the esteem and admiration of the public I, for one, have been a daily observer of the behaviour of a great number of your body of late, although I very seldom exchanged words with any of you, and can testify that your behaviour has been so far from evincing violence or disorder, that it deservedly claims the admiration of every friend of peace and order; and so little calculated to inspire fear or terror, that only souls already loaded with CRIME, or such as may, in the still and silent hour of night, be, like the great king of Babylon, troubled with the vision of their own blood-stained guilty consciences, they may see, or fancy they see, in the still watch of night, the meagre ghosts of the seventy-five persons who, on the 3d of May, 1815, were drowned in Heaton Pit!! Hush! what voice is that which, in deep, tremulous tones, exclaims, Murdered! murdered! murdered!! whilst each spectre appears to hold, with deadly grasp, in one hand, a fragment of putrid horse flesh, and with the other to present an expiring taper to some inscription chalked upon the lid of an *empty* candle-box!!!——Oh blood, blood, that hast a voice which reaches the throne of God! such persons as these may indeed be frightened at themslves, and seek the protection of soldiers' bayonets, and of cannon: but you, ye Pitmen, properly look to that eternal Being who says, "Vengence is mine, and I will repay it." Your conduct through the present trying time has, and I trust in God will continue to demonstrate your determination to "live peaceably with all men." Your daily amusements amongst yourselves may, and does enliven and animate the rural, rustic scenes of a country village, but never is or I trust will be, such as to give cause of alarm, even to your bitterest enemies.

Continue thus steadily united to regulate your conduct, and your countrymen and countrywomen will fight your battles for you without your interference. I regret to learn that it has been determined on amongst yourselves that no man is to go to work, even admitting his employers accede to and comply with his demands, until the whole body of the conspirators of Coal Owners do the same. With the greatest deference to your general counsels among yourselves, this I conceive a glaring error. First, from its tendency to keep up and support that systematic conspiracy of oppression and imposition so long existing among the Coal Owners. Secondly, from its denying support to those masters who may have, perhaps long and deeply, deplored your sufferings, yet dared not, as Members of the Conspiracy, to better your condition, for fear of the unhallowed censure of their brother conspirators. Let those gentlemen have your assistance; and do you work their work cheerfully, and you will thereby make a noble stroke at the yoke and fetters which are forged for you in the Councils of the Combination.

It is, in my view, acting ungenerously and ungratefully to those gentlemen who so readily offered to meet your wishes; therefore I presume to advise you to abandon this plan. Thirdly, were a half or a fourth part of you in good work, you could and would gladly contribute out of your weekly earnings, by way of *loan,* to the support of your less fortunate brethren, and thus narrow the circle of general suffering, and additionally satisfy the public that you are not that idle, disorderly, demi-savage crew, which your oppressors wish to represent you. In this light I view your resolution to be impolitic, and therefore not only advise you to abandon it, but likewise to seek employment in any other *way* or *place* you can obtain it, and thus strive to lessen your dependence upon your tyrant employers. I beg you to keep in mind that it is feared all your exertions may prove insufficient to protect you from charges of rape, robbery, plunder, murder, and other crimes and outrages; and that these may be committed with the knowledge, consent, and perhaps assistance of those upon whom they are committed, and witnesses may be suborned to charge the commission of those crimes upon you. Be, therefore doubly guarded in your conduct by night and by day, at home and abroad. To transport or hang a few of you would feast the savage eyes and hearts of your enemies. Be steady, therefore, but let no specious sophistry or pretences separate or disunite you as a body of men. Remember, "union is strength," and a bundle of twigs or sticks may bend, but are hard to break.

All the deep political knaves who have been, and wish to continue your oppressors, will put their entire genius in requisition, and blackest arts to work, to excite jealousies and suspicions amongst you, and they will try to deceive you by representing your best and warmest friends and wisest advisers as impostors, who intend to deceive you, and make a prey of you. Be guarded, therefore, on this point against the approach of the sappers and miners of the enemy.

But I would counsel you, to a man, to be doubly guarded against that individual amongst your own body who proposes to offer violence or injury either to the person or property of any man whatsoever. Such individual I would instantly suspect to be in the employ of the enemy, and a hireling who designed the ruin of your cause. And I would recommend such an one to be forthwith delivered up to the civil authorities, to be dealt with as the law directs. Let PEACE and ORDER be your motto on all occasions, for on this alone depends your ultimate victory.

Every day public feeling is and will continue to grow stronger in your favour, while you continue to conduct yourselves peaceably and orderly, but a common offence, committed by any one of your body, at this time, will be charged upon the whole, with all the aggravations and exaggerations which the "winged God of the Tyne," or the Durham fabricator and traducer can vomit from their gall-swollen hireling stomachs.

Many efforts may probably be made by your enemies to entrap some of you into a breach of the peace, and, after so entrapping you, they will then have what you have not hitherto given them, viz. a shadow of an excuse for calling out the soldiers, under the vain hope that you will be frightened into their measures. For those silly blockheads are actually not aware, that the brave soldiers are your friends; that they despise and execrate the tyrant oppressors, who drove many of them to abandon their "dear, their native home," and to exchange the pick for the musket; for although the situation of a brave soldier is a thousand-fold preferable to that of a Pitman, yet a military life is not congenial to every man's taste—hence nothing but the oppressions under which those youths groaned, drove many of them into the army.

Your oppressors, forgetting this, or rather wishing to forget it, vainly wish to overawe you by calling out many of your sons and brothers, armed with a gun and bayonet, to frighten you; whilst not only the brave soldier, but his very officer who commands him, bears public testimony to the justice of your cause; and if called upon to resort to coercive measures against you, might chance to point the musket rather against your oppressors than against the relatives of the very men they command. But do not you, as a body of men, presume upon any thing but the steadiness of your conduct for a successful issue to your present cause.—Therefore submit peaceably to injury, to personal insult, nay to imprisonment itself; but in no case lay yourselves open to any charge of having violated the peace or laws of your country.

All then that is requisite on your part at the present time is, "To stand still, and see the salvation of God."

May your case be a warning to tyrants for the future not to goad public feeling too deep, or to carry oppression too far; and that a new era may open in the Pitman's life, and the Pitman's condition and circumstances, is the spontaneous wish and ardent prayer of your disinterested friend, WILLIAM SCOTT.

P. S. Since writing the preceding pages I have learned that some of the dangers I have cautioned you against, of charges of rape, of plunder, nay of murder itself, have actually been made against you as a body; but your calumniators have been compelled to abandon those falsehoods, and their only reward for such charges is that indignant scorn and contempt which is poured upon them by a British public, who in general consider themselves insulted by the fabrication of such falsehoods, and the consequent attempt made by such means to excite public alarm.

I have also been told of a miscreant ruffian, of the name of Wood, (a viewer,) who daringly violated the laws of the nation by seizing hold of some of the Pitmen by the collars of their coats, in open day-light, when peacefully going on their business; and, in conjunction with three or four more of his brother tyrants, threatened to lodge an ounce of lead in one man's body, if he did not instantly go to and remain within his house.

FINIS.

J. Marshall,
Printer, Newcastle.

A

LETTER

ON THE

DISPUTES BETWEEN THE COAL-OWNERS & PITMEN,

ADDRESSED TO THE

EDITOR OF THE TYNE MERCURY.

LETTER, &c.

To the Editor of the Tyne Mercury.

IX. "Thou shalt not bear false witness against thy neighbour."
DECALOGUE.

SIR,

AS Mr Losh, in your paper of the 21st ult., has replied to *only a part* of the letter of "An Old Pitman," which appeared in the *Chronicle* of the 18th ult., I therefore send you the following few observations as an answer, if an answer it deserves, to the only remaining part worth notice, premising that I would be one of the last to lift a pen in any attempt, however feeble that attempt might be, to abet, encourage, or palliate any grievance or act of oppression imposed upon any class of individuals, much more so the industrious class of Pitmen, of which I have been one from my childhood; but as in their various publications or letters given to the Public they have generally shewn such an unblushing disregard to truth—such an evident design, by garbled and grossly-exaggerated statements, to mislead the Public, who generally know little or nothing of these concerns, but which amounts to a declaration of the palpable unjustness of their cause to people who really know the nature of the disputed points, that I think it blameable to let them thus continue imposing on the credulity and opinion of the Public without some little contradiction.

The only remaining unanswered part, then, of the said letter which I shall notice is, that about the putting, and which he denominates "worse than Egyptian bondage." Now, sir, I take the liberty of telling this old man that his scale of prices for putting is a *false* scale; and that *if it were true*, it is extended to an utterly impracticable length, and for a reason very apparent, doubtless, as usual, to excite a morbid sensibility in the public mind, by giving a magnified and distorted view, and imposing an appalling front on hardships that have no existence but in the imagination, *to make the shopkeepers pity their case.*

I say his scale of prices is false, inasmuch as he takes only the maximum or most extreme lengths before he has added another penny to the score price; thus, for example, when 80 yards is the exact average distance, the price is, as he states, 1s. 3d. per score; but if only half this distance, or even less, the price is still 1s. 3d. per score; and immediately after the average distance *passeth* or *exceeds* 80 yards, say 81 yards for instance, then the practice is, and which is explicitly declared in the bonds, to *add* one penny to the score price, making 1s. 4d. per score, which continues until the average distance exceeds 100 yards, and so on, adding one penny for every 20 yards further. Now this old loon in his calculations has taken the *most extreme verge* of renk, whence it is 19 chances out of 20, or 20 out of 21, but that his scale is utterly false. Again, the score price, as is well known, in ordinary situations very seldom exceeds 1s. 8d. per score, which is one penny per corf for the Tyne, and will make the Putter travel at the utmost $4\frac{1}{11}$ miles for 1s. 8d.; but it may happen that he travels but $3\frac{29}{44}$ miles for the same; consequently he will earn 5s. for travelling

$12\frac{3}{11}$, or 11 miles nearly, respectively, half of which distance is with an empty corf; hence he is paid 5s. for dragging a load of about $5\frac{3}{4}$ cwt. of coals $5\frac{3}{4}$ miles on a metal plate-way, whose average position may be fairly taken to be horizontal, which is 3s. $1\frac{3}{4}$d. and 2s. 10d. per ton per mile respectively, a mean of which is 3s. per ton per mile, and this too in the most extreme and unfavourable case, where an active youth of about 17 years of age can easily earn from 4s. 6d. to 5s. per day when at full work. In shorter renks it is more favourable, as in the first renk, where the price is 1s. 3d. per score, and the greatest average distance $1\frac{56}{44}$ mile, or $\frac{40}{44}$th part of a mile with the load, will give 4s. $9\frac{1}{2}$d. per ton per mile, a mean of which is 9s. 7d. per ton per mile. From this the Public may form their own conclusions about the Putters being so very badly paid, and whether, were the work above ground instead of underground, they would be able to continue such prices. But the greatest hardship imposed on the Putter, and which is far the hardest part of his "Egyptian bondage," is what neither this nor any other old Pitman has thought proper to inform the Public, namely, *working part of the Hewers' work,* which is *filling his coals*: ah! here's the rub. —Will this old man inform the Public what right a Putter has to fill frequently from 20 to 40 corves of coals per day? I have known them fill 50 corves for the Hewers without any payment. The bonds, or agreements, enjoin the Hewers' prices to be for *hewing and filling*, &c. &c. Yet these compassionate creatures, whose souls are so keenly alive and opposed to every species of tyranny and oppression, whose delicate, melting, sensibility shudders with abhorrence at the idea of oppression exercised even upon a fly, hesitate not to lay an unfair, unjust, and oppressive burthen on the poor Putter, which is worse than all his own work, whilst they themselves pocket the money, making each tram (so called) fill a quantity of coals equal to about 9 or 10 double-horse carts per day, or nearly 8¾ tons lifted about four feet high, or 35 tons lifted one foot high per day, with which he has no business, and without one farthing remuneration, but very likely *his thumps* next morning if he has neglected filling them all. What rank oppression! what gross injustice! what glaring inconsistency! It is this and such as this that so frequently *stints* the pit boy in his growth and renders him a "useless thing."

Having, as I think, sufficiently shown the falsity of the "Old Pitman's" assertions about putting, I would beg leave to ask all the grace-be-here humgudgeons and pigmy pit-O'Connells, who have and still continue to mislead and delude the thoughtless and unwary into crime and consequent punishment, and then have the effrontery to come publicly forward and protest themselves innocent, saying, had it not been for them, things would have been much worse, as they did all in their power to restrain violence, &c., but on whose long, solemn, and consequential faces, one may already observe a streak of crimson; I say I would ask them what they mean by unsettling men's minds by their preposterous and nonsensical doctrines, teaching them to consider their masters as ruthless tyrants, unreasonable and unjust task-masters, slave-drivers, &c., and designate honest labour to be worse than negro slavery, Egyptian bondage, &c., and decent servitude, unworthy degradation, abject dependance, slavish submission, &c., and put the unmeaning (in their case) words of liberty! independance! &c. into their mouths? I would also, as a sincere and disinterested friend, advise all the leaders, organizers, and promoters of the pitmen's union, combination, or conspiracy, to pause, and calmly consider whether the certain decrepitude, or contraction, if not the eventual utter ruin of the coal trade of this district, as well as their own ultimate and irreparable loss, which must ensue, will be adequately compensated by, or a fair equivalent for, any temporary advantage they may at present derive by such combinations, and to retrace their steps while there is yet time, for they may be certain that gentlemen who have large capital employed in the coal trade will withdraw such capital the first fitting opportunity, as the present exorbitant prices demanded and obtained will not afford a fair remunerating profit for the *great risk* of *serious loss*. And with all the cunning and stratagem used by such leaders, they can never alter the immutable law of all trade and commerce, that the price of labour, as of every other commodity, must always be in proportion to the scarcity or the abundance of the supply; and if, as they have done, they continue by combination to enforce any artificial price of labour above this natural standard, they infallibly accelerate the ruin of their occupation, and that with accumulated misery: let them paint their garbled statements an inch thick with falsehood and calumny, unto this complexion things must come at last.— All combinations, as well of the masters as of the men, public as well as private, ought to be put down by the strong arm of the law, and things always left to find their own level.

I am, Sir,

Your humble Servant,

CASTOR.

February 29th, 1832.

Printed by W., E., and H. Mitchell, Newcastle.

REPORT

BY THE

Committee of the Coalowners

RESPECTING THE

PRESENT SITUATION OF THE TRADE.

Coal Trade Office, Newcastle upon Tyne,
10th March, 1832.

AT a General Meeting of COALOWNERS of the Rivers TYNE and WEAR, held here this day,

It was unanimously resolved,

That the Report now read, as the Report of the Committee of the Coalowners, be adopted by this meeting, and that the same be printed, and published in the London and provincial newspapers.

ROBT. WM. BRANDLING,
Chairman.

REPORT, &c.

IN compliance with the general wish of the trade, the Committee have given their best attention to those disputes which have for some time past so frequently arisen between the Coalowners and the Pitmen, in order to discover whether the latter, as a body, have any just cause of complaint; and should it appear to be the case, to point out what, in the opinion of the Committee, would be the proper remedy.

The Viewers of the different collieries have furnished statements founded on their own personal observation, and an accurate examination of their fortnight pay bills, which are regularly kept; and from these it appears that two-thirds of the Hewers, from the period when they were engaged in May last, to the termination of the year, have obtained, without any extraordinary exertion, 4s. a day in six hours, and the remaining one-third the same sum in seven hours; the average earning of each able-bodied young man, or of two boys acting as Putters, has been 4s. in eleven hours; the regular wages of Shifters (who, from age or infirmity, are generally unable to hew) have been 3s. for eight hours; boys who drive the rollies have been paid 1s. 3d., and those who keep the trap doors from 10d. to 1s. per day, not exceeding twelve hours, the occupation of the Drivers requiring no great bodily exertion, and that of the Trappers merely attention. Eight hours in the day have always been considered as the customary day's work for a Hewer, whose labour necessarily regulates all other operations in the mine.

By the above statement it appears, that since their last engagement, the customary working hours have been considerably reduced, and the workmen acknowledge that this has taken place in consequence of a regulation amongst themselves, that no Coalhewer shall be allowed to earn more than four shillings a-day. By this restriction one-fourth less work has been performed by two-thirds, and one-eighth less by the remainder, than would have been executed had they remained the usual time in the pit. Calculating upon the quantity actually raised, the deficiency is 171,606 Newcastle chaldrons, which, added to the quantity that would have been produced during the time that the pits were off work, supposing the same quantity would have been raised in the corresponding period of 1831 as in the preceding year, gives a total of 317,-519 chaldrons, equal to 841,425 tons, which, at 18s. per ton, is L757,282. Assuming that only one-third of this quantity could have been sold (of which there can exist no doubt, from the actual vend and the time ships were kept waiting), the loss to the general trade of the district, and to the Colliers themselves, is sufficiently apparent.

The loss and inconvenience sustained compelled some of the Coalowners to introduce strangers as Workmen in their mines, in order to assist in raising a supply equal to the demand: this was resisted by the Pitmen, and many acts of violence and outrage were committed; these collieries were stopped for a time, but the Proprietors persevered, and procured a supply of labourers, by whom the works are now carried on. Upon enquiring of these Owners and their Agents, it is found that the new Workmen experience no difficulty whatever in performing the work—that they execute it well, and are perfectly satisfied with the nature of the employment and the wages they receive. These facts are most important, as they prove beyond the possibility of doubt, that the Pitmen formerly employed could have been neither overworked nor ill-paid—that it requires neither great skill nor any long previous training to become an expert Coalworkman, and that such labour is abundant and easily to be procured. The Committee feel, therefore, perfectly justified in declaring, that these disputes could not have originated in any real grievances, but must have been caused and kept alive by the Workmen, unfortunately allowing themselves to be persuaded that they could accomplish the object of securing constant work and high wages, by a secret combination to control the free circulation of labour.

That such a combination was not, as has been craftily pretended, in the nature of a benefit society, for the purpose of providing for the aged and sick, or to assist each other in obtaining the best price for their labour previous to entering into any engagements with their Employers, which, unaccompanied by any display of force or violence, is perfectly legal; but, that it was entered into in the vain hope of protecting themselves by their numbers whenever they felt inclined to set the law at defiance, has been clearly established, by the murderous attempts upon the lives of the Workmen, and felonious destruction of property at Waldridge—by the riots and outrages of various places in the two counties—by the money payments made from a general fund to those Pitmen who deserted their employment, or were discharged by the Magistrates, and by the threats and intimidation that have been used to induce individuals to join the general confederacy.

A candid perusal of the foregoing statement must convince every unprejudiced person that a supply of coals sufficient to meet the gradual increase of the trade, or any sudden demand, cannot be insured by a mere payment of liberal wages, and that mutual confidence and a good understanding can never be established, and a proper submission to the law maintained, by the Coalowners timidly abandoning their undoubted rights.—The Committee therefore most earnestly recommend, that in all agreements that may hereafter be entered into with the Workmen, the greatest care should be taken to render them as clear and comprehensive as possible, and perfectly explicit upon all points, wherein the least doubt or misunderstanding can possibly arise—that the decided and proper course adopted by those Coalowners who have successfully resisted the unlawful demands of the Pitmen should be pursued in all cases where they violate their voluntary engagements; and, above all, that immediate and effectual measures should be taken by the trade generally to secure to every individual complete indemnity for any loss he may sustain, in seeking protection and redress from the laws of his country.

Printed by W., E., and H. Mitchell, Newcastle.

AN

IMPARTIAL ENQUIRY

INTO THE

EXISTING CAUSES OF DISPUTE

BETWEEN THE

COAL OWNERS

OF THE

WEAR AND TYNE,

AND THEIR LATE

PITMEN.

BY SCRUTATOR.

"The fool foldeth his hands together, and eateth his own flesh." ECCLES. C. IV. v. V.

HOUGHTON-LE-SPRING:

PRINTED FOR THE AUTHOR BY J. BECKWITH.

1832.

TO

THE PUBLIC.

Ere I enter on the consideration of the disputes existing between the Collieries of the Tyne & Wear and their Employers, some slight avowal of the motives which induce me thus to address the Bar of Public opinion might be expected, and indeed is due to those to whom the following observations are addressed. To disabuse, then the Public mind, Impartially to state, and place in clear and intelligible light the points at issue, are the humble pretensions of those few pages. To remove the untenable grounds of dissatisfaction on which those misguided men now rest; and to promote the mutual good of the Employer and Employed is the earnest wish of the

Author.

JUNE 18th, 1832.

In order that I may render more intelligible and more fully consider the subject in its different bearings, it will be necessary first to take a brief and slightly retrospective view of the occurrences and disputes of the past year.

It must be fresh in the recollection of every one that the Pitmen in March 1831 demanded, and after a stop of Seven Weeks, obtained an advance in their wages of at least 30 per Cent, with several alterations in the general clauses of the Bond all in their favour, and thus by adjusting or removing all reasonable grounds of dispute, and advancing their rate of pay far beyond the average remuneration of ordinary Labourers, it was hoped by the Owners that all cause of future disagreement was thus removed; but what has the event proved? Have the Pitmen, after the concessions made to them of all their demands, renewed their labours and peaceably agreed to that Bond which granted them so many additional privileges? No! the reverse of all this has been the result; the granting of their former claims has but renewed the spirit of exaction which characterised the first Strike, and infused into their minds an exalted idea of their own power and consequence, which cannot fail to be alike injurious to the Owners and themselves.

An impartial observer, on examining the grounds on which the Pitmen now refuse to resume their work could not but be surpized that a body of men should still obstinately persevere in a course which must ultimately involve them in poverty and ruin, and even their late advocates must now condemn their acts which can tend only to the subversion of every Law and the cancelling of every bond which has hitherto held society together, viz. The relative power and superiority of the Master and his servant, to preserve which has been by all civil institutions deemed necessary to the preservation of the welfare of the community. For that this is the end proposed by the Pitmen is but two apparent; for on what do we now find their refusal to labour founded? Is it that fruitful source of dissension, the ill requital of their labour? The number of Hours ? or the much complained of degradation of their children? No! for all those have the Owners amended, almost on their own terms, and all that could affect the comfort of themselves or children has been granted by their Employers; but we find the continuance of their present "stick" depending on a cause which to all thinking men must be one less tenable and justifiable, viz. the refusal of the Owners to tolerate their League or Union, by which they foolishly hope to place themselves in future beyond the influence of their employers, and make themselves rulers over those whom they are bound to obey; for is it consistent that men who have hazarded thousands, nay, often risked their whole fortunes in undertakings often of dubious success, or is it right I would ask, that those men should succumb to the dictation of their workmen? It is but just and equitable, I grant, that the Labourer should receive a due and ample remuneration for his labour; and that he be left at perfect liberty to resort to those places and masters who offer the highest price for his labour; and further, I would wish the extension of all those privileges and immunities, consistent with their respective stations, which could tend to the improvement of their moral condition or the enjoyment of the comforts of life ; but labour as commodities, must be regulated by the proportion of the supply to the demand. If the supply be greater than the demand, the price must necessarily fall, and vice versa : for unless labour yield a profit to the Employer he must cease to purchase it. For the wages of labour must find their level in the market ; if its employment yield a fair remuneration to the Capitalist there will be a corresponding demand. If not, the Capital so embarked will be either withdrawn or soon exhausted. Such are the simple data on which we must found our criterion, and the standard by which must be tried the rate of wages the Pitmen have received. The question then to be determined, is one of easy solution.

Are the conditions which the Owners now have offered to their workmen such as afford a just remuneration. for their labour ? or tend to the removal of the grievances of which they complained ? and that the Public may form their own estimate of their pay, it is only necessary to state that the average period in which they can earn four shillings is only Six hours out of the Twenty four, and many of the most able bodied men can make it in Four hours.

Seeing then that their number of hours or the rate of their pay can no longer be a just cause of difference let us now revert to their last plea, and their supposed strong hold of objection, viz. the refusal of their Owners to acknowledge or admit of their Union. Of the Union I have already spoken generally and shall now enter a little into the details, and for that purpose examine a few of the clauses of its enactments. It is true the professed intention of the Union, or as they term it "The Coal Miners' Friendly Society" is to afford relief in cases of sickness or old age, but that this is only a minor consideration and its least important object, must be evident to every one who views the tenor of their late conduct or examines their Rules, which bear upon their very face opposition to the wishes and interests of their Employers.

Were it really what it professes to be, and its funds applied to the relief of the sick or the support of the aged, then I am assured every Coal Owner would gladly subscribe to the promotion of so desirable an object; but where we find it upholding the turbulent in unjust opposition to the interests of their Employers and of those of their fellow-workmen, who but for the species of intimidation which has been employed, would gladly resume their occupation, and where we see its funds given to support the Indolent in their unmanly slothfulness, then, I think, such a Society must meet with the decided disapproval of every peaceable and honest man. To shew the absurdity and dangerous tendency of this Union, I shall here state a few of the rules and regulations by which it is governed, And first the Seventh Article, which alone might suffice to shew its assumption of power and right of dictation.

"That if any Member of this Society have a desire to leave his Colliery to go to any other, he be required to get a Certificate from the Colliery he belongs to and lay it before the committee of the Colliery he intends to go to, before he goes to make a Bargain or agreement with the master he intends to agree with, or be excluded from the Society"

Now it is well known that this rule has been enforced to the fullest extent at Coxlodge and other Collieries where the Pitmen refused to go to work on account of men being employed who had not been thus duly *chartered ;* nay ! indeed, if any Colliery were ever so much in want of workmen the agents were deterred from employing any man unless he brought a Certificate from the Delegates giving the Agents leave to employ him. Nor have they stopped here, but have wished to assume a prerogative which hitherto none have dreamt of denying to the possessor of property viz. his choice of an Agent into whose hands he should trust its management, but we find the Pitmen, regardless of what all others have respected, have attempted to wrest even this privilege from the shackled Owner and offered,(obligingly enough)to take upon themselvesthe arduous task of selecting an agent whose *levelling* abilities should be commensurate with their own standard of perfection, and thus we actually find them at Hetton, the most extensive Colliery in the Trade, signing a document which they presented to the Owners demanding that the principal Viewer might be discharged, otherwise they would not hire on any terms, and they even refused to allow the Viewer to read to them the Terms proposed by the Owners.

I have already advocated the right of free agency which is the right of those as of other Men, and would also grant them the option of starving in disgraceful idleness or enjoying the fruits of honest labour on the advantageous terms now offered, but cannot go so far as to rest in their hands the right of controlling the actions of their Employers or of depriving them of that same free will in the selection of their Servants or the management of their property. The present "strike" of the Colliers has shewn that there is a point of concession beyond which it would be dangerous and ruinous to go: in fine, if the Thousands which are one day vested by a private individual are the next to be wrested from him, or governed by a lawless multitude, there is then an end to all law which can protect society. This is an "argumentum ad hominem" which affects alike the owner of a single acre or the possessor of the widest domains.

The next regulation of the Union which I shall notice is, the 8th. Article which says thus:—

"That no members of this Society earn more than Four Shillings per day, clear of fines and Offtakes, while employed as a Hewer, for each and every day, if practicable; and in case any Member being a Hewer, earn above 4s. per day, all such sum or sums so earned above 4s shall be paid into the Fund; and in case any Member do not well and truly state to the Committee of this Society the amount of his earnings, or shall either directly or indirectly defraud, or attempt to defraud, the Society of his said Earnings, or fines or forfeitures, in any or either of the said cases, such Member shall be fined double the Sum such Member shall have kept back, or be excluded"

It would be difficult to conceive a greater inconsistency than is afforded by the above regulation, or one more absurdly capricious and this too we find to be a regulation not imposed on but suggested by the very men who but a few weeks previous had railed so loudly against their inefficiency of pay; and I may state that at one period of last year this limitation of 4s. was by them actually reduced to 3s. to the manifest injury of themselves, their Employers and the public; the supply which was obtained on those terms being far short of the demand.

The last of their regulations to be considered is that in which is enjoined the good conduct of its Members and in which is set forth the punishment which shall follow the violation of the public peace, thus, "That all such members as shall bring disgrace upon this Fund by committing felony, or any other crime whereby they may be liable to punishment either from church or state, or any way not governed by the Rules of this fund, or found guilty of embezzling the money belonging to the Fund, for every such offence to be excluded".

The protection given to the rioters of Waldridge Fell and other places is a sufficient evidence of the rigidity with which this rule has been enforced!

Having now shewn what the Union of the Pitmen is and some of the evils resulting from such an Association, we may now see how far its claims extend of being what it professes to be viz "a Friendly Society". Few I think, on contemplating the atrocities committed at Hetton, where an unfortunate being, who had dared to resume his duty and remove himself from the Union, was shot by a member of this Society, I say, few can remember those things and reconcile them with friendship or humanity, or at least this is a species of philanthropy of which we have hitherto remained in ignorance but which the march of mind in the 19th. Century has been destined to reveal; it may be charitable in an instant to remove a fellow being from the cares and toils of life, or the part of a christian to send him unprepared before his Maker; but few, I think, would wish to share their goodness on terms like these, or hail a murderous Bullet as a messenger of good, No! we cannot but distinguish in such acts the fruits and works of such an association; for where men thus separate themselves from the community, and league together for the redress of imaginary evils, there ever will be generated a spirit of exclusion unfriendly to the well being of society, and worse when wicked designing or wrong thinking men at every meeting can work upon the feelings of a misguided multitude by the rehearsals of hardships, which if they exist at all are owing to themselves, and can dismiss them with passions roused and ripe for the committal of every outrage. None, I think, can fail to recognize as an effect of this Union the destruction of that peaceable and quiet conduct which in their former disputes called forth the praise, and entitled them to the sympathy of the Public in general; or fail to see in the disgraceful scenes which have lately taken place, the working of the reckless spirit it has roused; for can men, living in a Country whose boast is freedom and the observance of public decency and order, witness and not shudder at the scene which was lately enacted at Heworth at the burial of a Lead Miner, or who could have heard the yell of savage exultation which there 'rose o'er the Grave of a fellow-being, whose crime in their eyes was his having undertaken labour which they had refused, and not lamented the madness of those unhappy men.

In concluding I would briefly enquire into the causes which have operated on the Colliers still inducing them so long to persevere in the upholding of their union and consequent idleness. There is one opinion which has prevailed amongst them which has more than any other tended to this, which is that labourers brought from a distance, or who have been employed in other occupations, are totally unable to effect the working of the necessary quantity of Coal, and that the Owners must ultimately, by necessity grant their demands or cease the working of their Collieries Another & scarcely secondary cause is the influence of their Delegates and the dread of being injured by their associates in case of withdrawing themselves from the society. The first of those though a natural supposition is now shewn to be utterly unfounded and that the Lead Miners and other Strangers have succeeded, in many instances in working a quantity of Coal equal to that raised by any ordinary Pitman. It is then to the influence which their Delegates yet retain that is due the further continuance of the union. For that it is the interest of those Delegates to exert their utmost energies in keeping alive the present feelings of the pitmen must be apparent, for thereby hangs their support and with its cessation, they must see the blight of all their high blown hopes and the destruction of their ill judged plans.

It would be useless for me further to examine the present question, or the ultimate fate of such an Assosiation as the Union ; for it bears about it so many evidences of its own destruction, for surely we want not a more conclusive argument to prove its instability than the defection of its own members ; for Individuals are daily dropping from a League by which they have lost so much and gained so little, & hundreds would now gladly blot their names from the list of its members was it not for the unlawful & revolting threats by which they are deterred, yet I would add a word or two in conclusion to those misguided Men. They have already persevered too long in their obstinacy entirely to redeem themselves, & the immense number of strangers which have supplied their places must hereafter be an incumbrance whose weight they at present little dream of; Nor would I have them "lay the flattering unction to their soul" that they can whenever they please to resume their labor, at pleasure shake off this stone which they have hung round their own Necks: no! the Owners cannot then with justice dismiss men whom they themselves have sought, nor will those men readily leave a district, where they have found such plenty, again to seek their wretched Hut and scanty Food.

It is then, tho' at the Eleventh Hour, only by an immediate compliance with the conditions now offered by the Coal Owners that they can in part redeem themselves, for even as it is, hundreds must hereafter fail to find employment and have cause to curse the delusion under which they have laboured.

Scrutator.

FINIS.

James Beckwith, Printer, Houghton-le-Spring.

AN
APPEAL TO THE PUBLIC,
FROM THE
PITMEN OF THE TYNE AND WEAR.

"WHENEVER garbled and perverted statements are laid before the public in support of any cause, it is manifest that such a cause cannot be based on truth or justice; an axiom which experience has demonstrated to be never failing, and, in short, infallible." We are induced to make this observation from seeing a paper addressed to the "Pitmen on the Tyne and Wear," but by whom it is not known; "a document so replete with delusive and unfounded statements, and, we must say, with intentional misrepresentations relative to the disputes between the Coal-owners and the Pitmen employed in their collieries, that we feel it our duty, a duty which we owe alike to the public and the Coal-owners (we thank the writer of the paper for his suitable preamble to our case) to take upon ourselves the task of explaining the actual merits of the case. And we do so not altogether without the hope that a correct understanding of the subject on the part of the community will have a tendency to bring the differences which have unhappily arisen on this question to a conclusion, equally satisfactory to the parties most immediately concerned, and beneficial to the public at large."

The first thing that strikes the eye of the "dupes of designing men," is the final resolution of the Coal-owners. We are somewhat concerned that the Coal-owners should have acted so impolitic as to state to the public that they have come to their final resolution, as if they were Popes, or infallible men. Now if *final* signifies conclusive, how far they can justify their conduct towards us on this occasion, we will not presume to say; surely it is not generous, it is not humane, in fine, it is not what we expected to have heard from those who bear the character of gentlemen. It certainly does not become gentlemen to act with such domination over their fellow-creatures, who are the instruments of accumulating them princely fortunes, at the risk of their own lives.

Now these Northern Champions stand forth like a Goliah and defy the numerous hosts of Pitmen to combat them in the cause of liberty; but we behold a stripling come forward, named Public Opinion, and bearing down these gigantic Philistines, and compelling them to recant from their "final resolution" from necessity more than choice.

Now respecting the "garbled statements" of the Coal-owners, "that an able-bodied hewer be supplied with work to enable him to earn 14*s.* per week at the least," can be rendered futile and fallacious by the seventh article in the bond, we will shew when we come to that part of the paper; and as it respects the "boys' day's work to be 12 hours at the crane," we cannot see this to be that concession, which has been blown out before the public as a cloud of blessings ready to burst upon our heads, or which Mr. John Brandling seemed to lay before the bench of mediators in the court, when he talked about boys being only 12 hours in the pit in future. This is what we want,—12 hours in the pit—because boys are sometimes three quarters of an hour, and even an hour in the pit before work commences at the crane, therefore the writer of the address would do much better to cease talking on this subject, and let the day's work begin as soon as they begin to go down the pit.

We also object to the binding on the first Saturday of January. *First*, because it is a season of the year that is not congenial to us as a body of men for hiring in; now if they had talked about October, or our present time, we could have met them, but not in the depth of winter. When they passed this resolution they have not had that "sound and enlightened" mind which the writer of this paper seems to have had at the time when he wrote it.

Secondly, they would laugh in their sleeve to see those "artful and designing individuals, who are styled the delegates," trudging through the mud and the snow for three months seeking work, with little prospect of getting any, in consequence of their "daily meetings to which they resort to intimidate and coerce the subjects of their most savage and un-English barbarity."

Thirdly, it would cause a man to rent a room for one quarter of a year, and he might get work from some of those philanthropic masters who make such a "considerable pecuniary sacrifice," and "be provided with house and fire-coal at 7*l.* per annum at least;" still he would have to pay a quarter's rent at least, beside his great loss of work. That the writer of this paper may succeed in maintaining these acts of inhumanity we think is very unjust, and that the public can countenance such a gross perversion of humanity, and "of facts is altogether beyond belief."

"And that no alteration is necessary as to the size of the corf!!!"

That no alteration is necessary as to the size of the corf!!!—How! what do these "mighty chiefs mean?" Is it the 26 and 28 peck corves that we have to send 20 pecks to bank in; this surely is not what they mean when they say that "no alteration is necessary." We know they will not allow us to measure these unreasonable monstrous big corves, but we know that nine 20-peck corves and 12 pecks over fill a Newcastle chaldron of 53 cwt., and in many instances eight of these corves have filled a Newcastle chaldron of 53 cwt.; and yet these men (shall we say from motives of kindness and charity) say that no alteration is necessary; surely, we say again, there is oppression in this.

"And that the fines must remain as before, as a necessary protection to the owners against negligence or fraud." Now if these fines were only imposed for "negligence or fraud," there might be some excuse for them; but they are often exacted for accidents, which the men are unable to prevent, and, in a very arbitrary manner, against which there is no appeal. That the fines were originally instituted against "negligence and fraud," we never attempted to deny; and that many good institutions are prostituted to bad purposes also cannot be denied, and this is one. That fines are, in many cases, very arbitrarily exacted, no man concerned in the coal pit can deny; for he unfortunately has every-day experience of it. But it is a question whether the Coal-owners are fully aware of the gross impositions which are daily transpiring among their servants. We believe that these fines are not generally known among the Coal-Owners, because we believe the major part of them are most honourable gentlemen; but they leave their agents to transact their business, while they are spending their fortunes many miles distant; thus their agents, many of whom are part owners, may impose upon us fines arbitrarily, while these gentlemen who are expecting all the time that we (their servants) are living comfortably, by the reports that are given them from those agents, while at the same time we are oppressed by those illegal fines, to enrich themselves, and make them petty Coal-owners; and thus become the "Mighty Chiefs" of oppression in the North, and saddle it upon those innocent gentlemen who embark capital in order to promote trade and commerce in the country.

To give a correct statement of these fines would fill a large pamphlet, and had we sufficient means we would; but here we shall barely hint at them:—1st. Set-out corves for deficiency of measure let it be ever so little; and not unfrequently where the measure-tub is not at the pit's mouth, corves are set out when they are above measure, by reason of the unreasonable monstrous big corves, and yet they say that "no alteration is necessary." 2d. For foul coal, splent, stone, and small coals; if there be one quart found in a corf we are fined three-pence, two quarts sixpence, and if any of these ingredients amount to four quarts we are to be fined five shillings, or be guilty of a "misdemeanour, and be subjected to such penalty as may be inflicted by law," but rather than bring us to law they will sometimes lay on a penalty of ten shillings or twenty shillings!

But, in separation collieries, in case of four quarts of small coals being found in any one corf the hewer thereof is to forfeit one shilling; and yet these fines, they say, are inflicted for no other purpose than a "necessary protection to the Owners against negligence and fraud." Now, if we had open day-light in many instances we might avoid those evils, but by reason of the faint light emited by candles from forty to sixty in the pound, avoirdupoise weight, and in many instances the Davy lamp, it is impossible to avoid these evils, viz.: of getting the aforesaid quantity of "foul-coal, splent, stone, or small coals," and for fines of this kind we have from one shilling to four shillings to pay in the fortnight, *and it sometimes happens that we come to the bank in debt, after having wrought sufficient work for four shillings, the fines amounting to more than that sum.* We would ask any unprejudiced person if this is not oppression?

"That no Coal-owner carry on his colliery after the 6th of April with unbound men;" there certainly is some great advantage accruing to the Coal-owners from these productions of our oppressors denominated bonds; by them we become "dupes of designing men;" by them we are made tools for their purpose; by them we are either to work or lie idle; by them they are enriched; by them they are empowered with something like legal authority. According to the present construction of the bond we have little or no claim upon magisterial interference relative to disputes between them and us, but things of this nature are to be decided by two or more Coal-viewers.* Here are fine laws for men, yea, Englishmen, men that boast of liberty, and men that are endeavouring to put an end to West Indian slavery, to be governed by!

We next intend to notice the *second* and *seventh* articles, "The hewers are to be allowed during the whole period of their hiring, save for one fortnight at Christmas, *and in case of accident, as provided for by the seventh condition,* not less work than will yield to them, at the afore-mentioned rates, the sum of twenty-eight shillings; but if at any time the said Owners shall deem it expedient for the said hereby hired parties to work no more than nine days in a fortnight, the said Owners are hereby empowered to lay the pits off for the other days, allowing the hewers to earn in such nine days, not less than the aforesaid sum of twenty-eight shillings each."

Seventh, "That if by any accident happening to the engine, or from any other cause, a pit shall be rendered unfit for working, and the said parties hereby hired shall be laid idle for more than three successive days, two shillings and sixpence per day shall be paid to such of the said parties as are hewers, one shilling and sixpence per day to such of them as are putters, and sixpence per day to such of them as are drivers, provided that they work at any other

* Thus Coal-viewers are our accusers, judges, and executioners, and we have no mediators, or no other court to which we have access; but what they say and do are the laws by which we are coerced, and not the laws of our nation.

labour offered to them by the said Owners, &c., and, in case such work is not provided for them, and in case they are permitted by the said Owners, &c. to find employment elsewhere, and that such employment may be had, then the hewers shall receive only one shilling and sixpence per day, putters nine-pence, and drivers fourpence per day each; and, in the event of any of the said parties being, with the permission of the Owners, fully employed in any other colliery, no payment whatever shall be made to them during such employment."

Here the Coal-owners have published the banns of marriage between the second and seventh articles in the bond, and they ought to have said—If any of the Pitmen know cause or just impediment why these two articles should not be joined together in holy matrimony they are to declare it; this is the first time of asking. We, the Pitmen, declare we know cause and just impediment why they should not be joined. First, we are to have twenty-eight shillings, save for one fortnight at Christmass, and, in case of accident, as provided for in the seventh condition, and this seventh condition expressly declares that if by any accident happening the engine, or from any other cause, a pit shall be rendered unfit for working for three days, on the fourth we are to have two shillings and sixpence per day if they give us any other work, and if it can be proved that *no work can be got at any other place, we are to have nothing;* and eleven days at nothing per day does not amount to 28*s.*; but suppose it can be proved we can get work elsewhere, and our masters have no work either at bank or in the pit, and will not quit us, we can demand, according to the seventh article, only 1*s.* 6*d.* per day; and eleven days at 1*s.* 6*d.* per day is only 16*s.* 6*d.*, and this is not 28*s.* And again, if the pit is not fit for working, or if any thing happens to the engine, and the master should find us work above bank, we can only demand 2*s.* 6*d.* per day for eleven days, which is only 27*s.* 6*d.*, and this is not 28*s.* So these are the causes and impediments we have that these two parties ought not to be joined in holy matrimony, but we think they should be put out of the world, for we can do better without them than with them, lest such monsters should produce in the world a progeny of greater monsters, and devour us poor Pitmen.

The thing that will first strike the mind of any unprejudiced person will be, the obvious and undeniable truth that the representation contained in the address published on the part of the pitmen in the Chronicle, for April 9, that we may not be prevented from earning from seven to nine shillings per week, at the arbitrary will of the coal owners, is a declaration that can be founded upon past experience with sufficient grounds to anticipate the same in future, so there is no reason for any man to be "astonished how either us or the delegates attempt to impose upon the public;" it is not us, it is the Coal-owners. It is quite clear that the first resolution passed at the Coal-owners' meeting, is no guarantee to the Pitmen that they shall not receive less than 14*s.* per week, and that the statement given in the paper, addressed to the Pitmen of the Tyne and Wear, where the deductions were estimated at 1*s.* 8*d.* is a downright falsehood, which many of the Coal-viewers can prove, and have proved to be so; had he said from 3*s.* to 10*s.* he would be nearer the mark. The writer of the address states the minimum at 14*s.*, but there are some collieries on the Tyne have had their maximum at 14*s.* per week. He talks of there being a brisk coal trade seven or eight months in the year. There are some collieries have not wrought above three quarters of the year; and, in some cases, only wrought six or seven days in three weeks, so here all his logic falls to the ground.

It is a notorious fact that there does not exist at present a sufficient number of Pitmen, if the work were to be done regularly as with other labourers and mechanics, because one Pitman does nearly as much work as two men in any other branch of business or calling; and if many labouring men were to work to the extreme that a Pitman does, they would earn thirty shillings per week!!! The statement that our houses and firing are worth seven pound per annum at least, is surely a hoax on the public, as many of our houses are not worth four pounds per annum.

From the statement we have thus made, the owners may, we think, very truly be denounced as hard taskmasters; but we leave it to the public to decide between us. That it is reasonable on our part to insist on an increase of wages, is evident from what has gone before, and from the repeal of the coal duty, and from the princely fortunes the Coal-owners and their viewers or agents are making, in connexion with the dangers we undergo, are sufficient reasons we will leave the public to judge. The assertion that we resort to intimidation and coercion towards those who are willing to accept the terms offered them, is not true; and if we have "gained the ascendancy over the timid and mild, and especially over the youths," it is what our lordly masters have done for many years. And if we have almost daily meetings, what business have our masters with it, so long as we don't meet to injure them or their property,* but to devise means whereby we are to extricate ourselves and the rising generation from the galling bond of slavery; and instead of reproaching Ranter preachers, they ought to encourage and reward them for the judicious manner they have conducted themselves in, and endeavoured to restrain others from committing acts of violence. Had it not been for the Ranter preachers, in connexion with religious men in

* Experience is the school of wisdom, and fools will learn in no other; now this is the school we have learned to meet almost daily in, by reason of seeing the Coal-owners and their agents meet almost daily. This led us to think that there certainly was some extraordinary advantage accruing from these meeting, so we have tried the experiment for no other purpose.

other denominations, many of the Coal-viewers would not have had the opportunity of getting forward with such arbitrary means, and especially with the address now at issue; many of the "dupes," as they have termed them, would have risen had they not been constrained by argument by these men, whom they contemn so much, when the address was read containing so many untruths.

They say that, "immediately after the meetings break-up, parties go to the houses of the absentees, who are maltreated for disobedience to the mandate of their mighty chiefs."

What opprobrious language is this from men that are denominated gentlemen. It appears that this language may be very appropriately applied to our masters, for it is no way applicable to us as a body of men. Immediately after their meetings break up at Newcastle, parties go to the collieries; those that are disobedient to the mandates of our mighty chiefs are maltreated, fined, and their furniture thrown to the door, and our names circulated round the collieries as ringleaders and agitators of the timid and mild, who are anxious to continue bound slaves to a set of over-ruling tyrants. And as it respects the colliers' wages in the south, we believe that they have much more regular and better wages than we have, and at the same time work with great flannel shirts on like a ploughman; so don't contrast those Pitmen with the Pitmen in the north; and what comparison is there between the lead-mines and coal-works? If the lead miner finds a good vein, he perhaps gets as much in a quarter of a year as a Pitman does in a year. But here the writer of the pamphlet wants to intimidate us by talking about the magistrates adopting measures to preserve the public peace, when there never has been any peace broken by the body of Pitmen. Some individuals certainly have made violation of the peace, but the body of Pitmen are not to be reproached for that; and we must beware, "lest these wicked and designing men, or the unfortunate beings whom they delude and betray to the commission of acts which they must expiate on the scaffold." Poor fellow, if he had his own way he would hang all the Pitmen, and then his gains would be all at an end.

NEWCASTLE: PRINTED BY
T. AND J. HODGSON, UNION-STREET.

REPORT

OF THE

TRIALS OF THE PITMEN

And Others,

CONCERNED IN THE LATE

RIOTS, MURDERS, &c.,

IN THE

Hetton and other Collieries,

AT THE

Durham Summer Assizes, 1832,

INCLUDING A FULL REPORT OF

MR JUSTICE PARKE'S CHARGE

TO

THE GRAND JURY.

DURHAM:
PRINTED BY R. STOBBS.

DURHAM SUMMER ASSIZES, 1832.

MONDAY, July 30.

The Grand Jury having been sworn,

Mr Justice PARKE proceeded to charge the Grand Jury to the following effect:—

He looked forward with very painful feelings to the discharge of their duties and his own on the present occasion, in the administration of the criminal justice of the country for this county; and he did so not merely because the number of cases that would be brought under their consideration were unusually—he believed unprecedentedly—great, for this county, but because he perceived so many acts of violence against the persons of individuals, in which the lives of some of our fellow-creatures had been lost, and, if the evidence should be sufficient to bring home the guilt of the parties accused to their satisfaction, the lives of others must be sacrificed. All such cases demanded from jurors the most serious and attentive consideration. Another very painful consideration arose out of the depositions in the cases contained in the calendar that were now before him—namely, that almost every act of violence—he believed he would be right in saying every such act—might be directly attributed to those combinations amongst workmen which had prevailed in this country for a long time, and to a great extent—perhaps in this and the adjoining county to a greater extent than in any other part of England. These combinations unfortunately derived their origin from the change which took place in the law about five or six years ago. At that time, an Act of Parliament was passed, by which all the penalties upon combinations were repealed, and permission was afforded to workmen to meet for one purpose, and for one only, but which, he feared, they had made the cloak for other purposes which were unquestionably illegal. These combinations, which were dangerous to the commercial prosperity of the country—injurious to the peace and welfare of society—and injurious also to the persons concerned in them, must, one day or other, be put down. He hoped this great object might be accomplished by the law as it stood; and he was sure he would have the concurrence of all concerned in the dispensation of the laws—both of magistrates and of jurors,—when he said that an end so desirable would be largely promoted by their firm and fearless, yet temperate and impartial, exercise of the functions with which they were respectively invested. He would not detain them by any lengthened observations upon the cases in the calendar: the principles of law, as these were applicable to the various cases, would be too well known to them to render it necessary for him to offer any instruction to them as to the general nature of their duties. Two cases in the calendar were those which were of the greatest importance. One of these related to the death of Mr Fairles, and the other to that of a person who appeared to have filled the office of a private constable or watchman at Hetton. The crime of murder, his Lordship observed, would be committed when violence produced death, whether the object of the party inflicting that violence was to murder, or merely to do some grievous bodily harm. To constitute the offence, it was necessary they should be satisfied that the violence was committed with what the law called a *malus animus*—that is, with a heart regardless of social duties and deliberately bent on mischief; and whether they might entertain any doubt as to what the intention was,—whether to kill or not,—still if they should be of opinion that the violence produced grievous bodily harm, from which death ensued, the crime of murder would be made out. With respect to the other case, it appeared from the depositions before the Magistrates and the Coroner, that the deceased met with his death at midnight, from one or more gunshot wounds; and they would have a very laborious duty to investigate all the circumstances of the case, and to ascertain whether they were such as would lead to a moral conviction of the guilt of the persons accused, or any of them. It appeared that this murder—for murder it was—was committed in the presence of several individuals; and it was one proof of the demoralising consequences of such combinations that those individuals were either aiding in the murder, or were restrained from coming forward to disclose the facts against the persons by whom it was committed. His Lordship hoped, however, that, by a careful consideration of the circumstances of the case, they would be able to arrive at a just conclusion. —In allusion to a case of cutting and maiming, his Lordship said it was not necessary that the wounds should be inflicted by a sharp instrument; for if they were inflicted by a blunt instrument, and with intent to murder, or to do any grievous bodily harm, the offence, under the 9th of Geo. IV., would be completed. In another case, it would be necessary for them to consider whether the object of the persons charged,—who were persons connected with the Trade Union,—was merely to disturb the inhabitants of a dwelling house who were willing to work at the prices given by the masters of the collieries, or whether their intention was to kill the inmates, or to wound or do them some grievous bodily harm. If they should not think the parties had one or other of the latter objects, it would be their duty not to find a bill, and they might be indicted for the lesser offence of a common riot, as there appeared to have been more than three persons engaged in the transaction.—Before he dismissed them to their duties, it might be fitting he should mention to them, that since they were last assembled here on a similar occasion, the law had undergone two important alterations, in furtherance of the spirit in favour of the diminution of capital punishments which was prevailing in the country. The first of these alterations was made in May last, and the other in the present month of July. By the former, the punishment of death was taken away in reference to every species of coining; and by the second, from an offence very common in this and other agricultural counties—that of horse and cattle stealing. The punishment substituted for the former offence was transportation for life, or for 7 years, or (as we understood) for a period of imprisonment at the discretion of the Judge. But in the latter case, the Legislature had thought right to restrict the discretion of the Judges, and to fix the punishment at transportation for life—the object being to prevent the commission of the crime by providing a positive punishment, instead of leaving convictions uncertain while a heavier punishment obtained. Every well-wisher of his country must be gratified by the prevention of crime; and if, on experience, this change should be found to have a beneficial operation, a great point would be gained, in the correction of the evil of which it was intended to furnish a remedy.—The learned Judge then desired the Jury to proceed to the performance of their duties; and concluded by assuring them that if, in the discharge of these, any difficulty should present itself, he should cheerfully render them all the assistance in his power.

CUTTING AND MAIMING AT SHERIFF'S HILL.

ELIZABETH PARKIN, aged 50, WM. PARKIN, aged 20, THOS. VARTY, aged 21, ISAAC WALTON, aged 21, and JOSEPH ELLIOTT, were charged with assaulting Thomas Thew, with an intent to murder him or do him some grievous bodily harm.

The prosecutor, Thomas Thew, a pitman at Sheriff's Hill Colliery, had been a member of the Colliers' Union, but on going to work was expelled from that body. About 11 o'clock on the night of the 19th of May last, he went into the Three Tuns public house, near that place, in company with other two men. The prisoners, Wm. Parkin and Varty, were there. He had not been many minutes in the house when they each threw a stone or brick at him, and hit him on the left side of the head, and he got up and left the house immediately. He was afraid to go home by the turnpike and turned down Kell's Lane. He was about 20 minutes in the lane. When he got to an opening in the wall, at the end of Sheriff's Hill Row, 10 or 12 men and women rushed out upon him and knocked him down, and beat him severely with sticks. He recognised all the prisoners among the company, but could not say that Walton and Elliott struck at him. Elizabeth Parkin gave him the last blow he received, with a stone tied into a stocking, and he stooped down and stopped his breath, and she said, "D——n him for a beast," or "for a b———r, he's done now; that has done him," and then they all left him. He had a wound on the left side of his head, four inches long, and there was another incision above his right eye, and his hands were very much injured. He laid on the ground a little while, and then got up and made for home, but when he had got a little way on the road, he found himself very weak, and went to the pit to lay down. When he got there he met George Charlton, the watchman, who set him home. He told his wife the names of the persons who had ill-used him. He was four weeks and three days off work. On his cross-examination he admitted that he had a good deal of ale previously, but he was not at all drunk. A surgeon was called to depose to the nature of the wounds. On examination, he found the skull laid bare by the wound on the left side of the head and on the forehead. He considered him in great danger of his life from the fever and delirium that arose from the wounds and the loss of blood. On being cross-examined, he said that the drink might add to the fever, or might possibly cause delirium; but the blows were quite sufficient to cause fever without drink.

For the defence, witnesses were called to prove an *alibi*, in favour of Elizabeth and William Parkin and Varty, and several witnesses were called to speak to their characters.—Parkins and Varty, Guilty; and Walton and Elliott, Acquitted.

ROBBERY AT HETTON.

ROBERT WELSH, aged 27, and HENRY KENNEDY, aged 27, two Pitmen belonging Hetton, were arraigned for robbing James Napier, a Police-man at that place. Welsh pleaded guilty; but Kennedy put himself on his trial.

Mr Losh stated the case for the prosecution to the effect detailed in the following evidence; and Mr Ingham called

James Napier, who said,—I am one of the special constables employed at Hetton Colliery, and was at Barnfather's public house, at Elemore Vale, between 8 and 9 o'clock on the Sunday evening. Another special constable, named Dodds, and I went into the parlour. Welsh came in, and said there were two Union men out of doors—that he was frightened of his life, and wanted me to set him home. He said so a second time about 10 o'clock. Kennedy was there. I went with Welsh in consequence of this. When I went with Welsh, Kennedy and another man went with us. We went down a lane to a bridge, and then across the fields towards the Brick-garth. When we went along the lane, Welsh, the other man, and I went into a field through which there is a footpath parallel with the lane, and Kennedy went into the lane. We came upon the lane again, and then joined Kennedy. We went 50 yards along the lane till we came to a thorned gate. We got over, and went into another field, which we crossed—also a second; and then into a third, which was an oat field. Kennedy was on my right, Welsh on my left, and the other man behind. Our reason for being there was, that Welsh said he lived in a house at the corner of the field. When we got within 20 yards of a house in a corner of the field, the third man said "Bob, you don't live here now—you have been turned out, and live at the top of the lane." We turned from the house, and after getting about 150 yards up a footpath leading towards Easington Lane I was knocked down. Just before that, Kennedy was still on my right hand, Welsh on my left, and the other man behind me. I could not say for a certainty who knocked me down; but I think it was him who was behind me. I jumped on my feet. I caught hold of Kennedy and knocked him down, and was then thrown a-top of him. I felt a hand in my pocket, and saw Welsh jump upon my ear, with his two heels. Kennedy was still under me. I had three sovereigns and 2s. 6d. in my pocket. I could not make out whose hand it was. After Welsh jumped on my head, I cannot say what happened. I was knocked stupid, and cannot tell what number of blows I had afterwards. It might be about a quarter to 11 o'clock then. When I came to myself, I went up to a stile, and found I was in the wrong road. I turned 'round, and on feeling for my money I found it was gone. I went to Barnfather's and asked him who the men were; and he said Kennedy was one. I did not get in at Barnfather's, but went to the Police Station-house. Dodds and I had only two pints of porter between us, and I had a glass of whisky. The other men were not very drunk. When I paid the reckoning I took out all my money.

Cross-examined by Mr Archbold.—I was in this Court once before; I then stood in the dock. I was tried for felony, and was confined 16 months; but that is not what I am here for to-day. I am now a special constable, having been advanced from a prisoner to that dignity. The landlord saw my money. He is here to-day. I know a man of the name of Temple. I did not tell him there were only two men with me. I did not tell him I did not know how I lost my money. I did not accuse a man named John Dixon of this robbery.—He was not taken into custody on my information. I did not say I would swear to him till Barnfather said I was mistaken, and he was then discharged.

By the Judge.—Five or six men were taken and discharged on being brought to the Station-house.

A little man named John Dixon was here produced.

Witness.—I will swear I did not say I would swear to his being one of the men who robbed me. We were walking through the fields from a little after 10 till a quarter to 11. The lane Kennedy went down leads into Easington Lane, where his wife's father, I suppose, lives, and that would be his way home. I know it was past 10 o'clock, because the landlord said it was past 10, and he would fill no more drink. I know it besides from its being just in the dusk of the evening.

Re-examined.—When Dixon was at the Station, he was shewn to me along with several others, who were discharged when I could not recognise them. Temple is a brakesman employed in the engine. I went to his house to get a leech put on my eye; but had no conversation with him about the number of men who were with me. When I was at the Station-house, I described the third man to have had sandy whiskers,—that he was pock-marked, and had lost one of his front teeth.

Mr Martin Barnfather, the landlord of the public house, said the prosecutor came to my house about 9 o'clock. The two prisoners and some other men were in at the time. The prisoner was in the parlour at the other end at first; but he afterwards came into the kitchen, where the prisoners were, to light his pipe, and had some conversation with them, but I don't know what about. They drank to him, and he drank with them. Napier paid for a quart of ale they had, and also showed some sovereigns, but how many I cannot tell. The prisoners were in the same room, but I cannot tell whether they saw the sovereigns. I don't know how near they were to each other. They went out together. Welsh either said he had been bound or was going to get bound: that he was afraid to go home, and insisted upon Napier setting him home.—Napier said he had no objection. As they were going out of the door, Napier asked if he was safe—if the men he was going out with—these two men and another—would do him any harm? and I said no, I thought not. This was between 10 and 11: it was past 10, and I was going to shut up. I shut up at half past 10 at the latest, and it would be near that as well as I can guess. They went out, but I did not see which way they went. I did not observe any of them to be in liquor; Napier had taken nothing to make him so. Napier came back between 1 and 2 o'clock, to enquire the names of the men. He said they had almost murdered him, and he would come back in the morning to get their names. He said he knew Kennedy.

Cross-examined.—Kennedy did not remain at the door talking with me when they went out. I am quite sure he did not; for I shut the door and did not see which way they went. He did not say any thing as he passed out. Atcheson, the last man who went out, said "Good night."

Robert Wintrop, a special constable at Hetton, said he met Kennedy, on the night in question, between 12 and 1, between Mrs Smith's public house in the Brick-garth and Easington Lane. I was on sentry, and asked him what he had been about. He said he had been getting a drop of drink. I said "You are in a sad state"—for he appeared to be very much *clartied;* and he said he had been tumbling. I told him I would put him a button or two in his waistcoat, and did so. I asked him where he lived, and he said at Snipper's Gate. I told him it was time he was at home, and he bid me good night and went on. Napier came up about 10 o'clock; he was in a very bed state, all dirty and bloody: his left ear and right eye were severely bruised and cut.

Cross-examined.—Kennedy was drunk; he could walk, but was so drunk as to be in a tumbling state.

By the Judge.—It might be rather better than a quarter of a mile from Barnfather's where I met him, and about a mile from Snipper's Gate.

Mr Stephenson, clerk to the magistrates at Houghton, proved the examination of Kennedy, in which he said he never was with the prosecutor after coming out of Barnfather's, but went to Mrs Smith's, where he got a gill of ale, and afterwards fell into one of the brick-garth ponds.

Elizabeth Nicholson, the mother of Kennedy's wife, said I live in Easington Lane. Kennedy once lived with me. He did not sleep at my house on the night Napier was attacked. He was then biding at Snipper's Gate.

Cross-examined.—Snipper's Gate is near Easington Lane.

Mr John Anderson, of Hetton, deposed to the correctness of a plan of the localities connected with the transaction. It appeared that the road Kennedy took would lead both to Easington Lane and Snipper's Gate.

By the Judge.—Smith's house is to the north and Snipper's Gate to the south of the road leading from Easington Lane.

By Mr Archbold.—Kennedy's father lives in the Brick-garth.

Mr Edgar, surgeon, at Hetton, said I attended Napier on the Monday morning. He complained of a pain in his head; he was much bruised on his left ear and cheek, and also on his right eye. The bruises seemed to have been caused by some hard substance. There was also a bruise on his breast. I attended him till he resumed his occupation, which was in about four or five days.

By the JUDGE.—Though he was much bruised he was not dangerously hurt.

This was the case for the prosecution.

Kennedy, on being called upon for his defence, said he had nothing to state, except that his fellow-prisoner could clear him of the charge.

Mr ARCHBOLD called

John Dixon, who said I am a pitman. I was taken, for this robbery, to the police station, on Tuesday the 12th. The policeman who took me asked Napier if he knew me, and he said " Yes." " Was this one of the men ?" " Yes." " Would he swear it ?" " Yes." Barnfather was then sent for, and when he came, they asked him whether he knew me. He said " Yes ;" and they then asked him whether I was at his house on the Sunday. He said " No ;" and I was discharged.

Cross-examined.—Kennedy and Welsh were not there then. They were committed the day before. I don't know that I am the man who was suspected of being the third person.

John Hutton said, I live at Easington Lane. On the Sunday night, I saw Kennedy about 200 yards from Barnfather's. He was on the road, going home at Snipper's Colliery. I asked him where he had been, and he said at Barnfather's. I asked him who he was with, and he said he had been with Welsh. I asked him where Welsh had gone to, and he said he had gone away with the police.

Mr Justice PARK.—I don't know how you can make that evidence.

Mr ARCHBOLD.—To shew he was going home as he stated in his examination.

Witness.—That was between 10 and 11.

Cross-examined.—Kennedy said he was going to Smith's, to get a gill of ale. I was not one of the men who was taken up on suspicion of this robbery. [The witness's personal appearance bore a strong resemblance to the description given by the prosecutor of the third man at the station-house.]

Re-examined.—Kennedy and I walked on the road after that, as far as Smith's, which is in a garth off Easington Lane.

By the JUDGE.—I overtook him. I had been at Pittington. I had not been at Barnfather's. I want one of my fore teeth. I lost it a long time since.

Napier, on being recalled by the Judge, said I think that is the third man ; but I would not like to swear to him. At the station-house I said the man had sandy whiskers, was pockfritten, and had a tooth out before.

Barnfather (recalled) said, the witness is not one of the men who was drinking in my house. The three men went out of the house together. I knew him very well. He is a pitman, and lives at Easington Lane. He has not been out of the country at all.

John Speedy said, on Tuesday night, between 11 and 12, I saw Kennedy in the brick-garth, between Smith's and Easington Lane. He had just left witness and Best, two police men, when I saw him. I saw him no otherwise in his clothes than he is now. He had no mud on his breast then : if he had, I must have seen it.

Cross-examined.—He did not appear as if he had fallen into a brick-pond.

Re-examined.—He had not come to the brick-pond then. He had passed some; but he would have to pass others in going from Smith's to his wife's mother's.

By the JUDGE.—He had left Wintrop at that time.

By Mr ARCHBOLD.—I saw him leave them.

Edward Temple.—I am a brakesman at Hetton. I am not one of the men who has been out of employment. I saw Napier the morning after this affair. He was coming my way, and I called him in. I asked him what was the matter with him. He said he had been badly used by two men. I asked him where, and he told me in a field, which I knew by the description he gave me. He said he would not have cared about being badly used if he had not lost his money, but he could not tell where or how he lost it. I asked him if he found any of the men have their hands in his pocket, taking his money out, and he said "No, he knew nothing about it."

Mr ARCHBOLD.—I believe, Temple, we've been obliged to subpœna you

The witness assented.

By Mr INGHAM.—He said he had been ill-used by two men.

By the JUDGE.—I cannot tell whether two men were in custody at that time: it was about 5 o'clock on the Monday morning that he called.

Mr ARCHBOLD here proposed to examine Welsh in support of Kennedy's case, submitting that though the former had pleaded guilty, yet, as judgment had not been pronounced against him, he was, in law, a competent witness.

Mr INGHAM objected to this course; but

Mr Justice PARKE, on the authority of a case in which Mr Justice Le Blanc had pursued a similar course, decided that the testimony of Welsh was admissible.

Welsh was then sworn, and he said,—When we left the public house on the night in question, with Napier, a man named James Atcheson went along with me. Nobody else went. Atcheson and I went along with Napier; but Kennedy did not go along with us at all. I have pleaded guilty of this robbery; but Kennedy did not go five yards from the door with us, and was not present at the robbery.

Cross-examined by Mr LOSH.—Kennedy was in the public house with us; but he stopped to go to the low side of the house for a particular purpose. He did not accompany me. He would not go five yards in the direction to his home. He only went three or four yards to the low side of the house.—Kennedy did not go five yards into the lane from Barnfather's. I crossed on to the road, but he did not follow me. It was not true that he went five yards with me. He did not accompany me at all, and I did not see him after he came out of the house. We went over into the fields over a thorned-gate. Three of us went over that gate—Napier, Atcheson, and myself. I was very tipsy, and don't know when I came back to the lane. We never crossed the lane till after the robbery. I cannot say how many fields we went over, whether two or three. I don't know who gave the directions about going over the fields. I told Napier I was afraid of two men. I told Napier I was bound, but that was an untrue representation. I was going to be bound; but I never went to seek after it.

I had no reason for telling him I was afraid. I mentioned in the house that I would be bound next day if I lived. After we crossed the thorn gate, Napier went in the middle, I on his left, and Atcheson on the right. Atcheson is a little man; I know him well, but don't know his teeth or his hair. Atcheson had nothing to do with the robbery. I got the money. Napier was lying when I got it; but not upon any body. I knocked him down, and Atcheson struck him. I did not see Kennedy till next morning in the watch-house. He heard there was a warrant out against him, and he came and delivered himself up. I did not tell this story when it happened. Kennedy and I were locked up together. I said nothing of it then, either to the magistrates or any body else. I first mentioned it in gaol, to the chaps there. Kennedy and I were not in the same room together in gaol. I have said this before to-day; but I never told the Governor, nor any body who came to the gaol.

By the Judge.—I lived in Easington Lane; but the way we went, over the thorned gate, was not my way home. Nobody said it was not. I did not say I lived in a small house through that field. No man said "Bob, you don't live there—you're turned out." I recollect saying "Oh yes, I am—I live at the top of the lane." I did not live at the top of the lane. There was no man walking behind Napier. I cannot say whether Atcheson is marked with the small pox, or has sandy whiskers, or lost a tooth. I don't recollect that he said "Bob, you don't live there—you are turned out." I had not seen the money Napier had at the public house; but I felt for his money because I thought he had some upon him. I don't know what has become of Atcheson. I had made no agreement with him that we were to rob the man. The money was hid in the hedge in the field. It was not dark, but nobody saw me hide it. Atcheson was on before and did not see me hide it.

Re-examined.—The public house is on the right hand side before you go into the lane leading to Easington Lane. He went into the lane for a particular purpose. Those were the five yards I meant into the lane. I said I would be bound next morning; but I was taken at five o'clock on Monday morning, and have been in custody ever since. Kennedy heard there was a warrant out against him, and came and delivered himself up.

Welsh was here ordered to retire into the dock.

Napier was re-called by the Judge.—He said I am sure three men went over the fields, and were at the robbery. The third man had accompanied us all the way from Barnfather's, and was in there with us, and drank with them. I don't know Atcheson. We talked to Kennedy after meeting him again on the road; I am sure of that. Welsh got over the thorned gate first, I next, Kennedy third, and the other man last. I walked with him through the three fields, and we talked the whole way: I mean to Kennedy. I did not know his name at that time. I saw Kennedy in the lane before we got over at the thorned gate. I saw him at the gap where Welsh and I came into the lane; and we walked with him 50 or 60 yards to the gate. There was a footpath in the field we got into that led into Easington Lane. I have no recollection of having had any conversation with Edward Temple about the third man. I went to get a leech put upon my eye. I saw him about five o'clock. I did not tell him I did not feel any one's hand in my pocket. I would not tell him any thing at all about it. I did not see Kennedy attempting any thing. He was still standing on my right hand when I caught hold of him; and I know no more of the part he took beyond what I have told you. I don't know whether Kennedy struck me at all: I never saw him do so.

The learned JUDGE then summed up with great clearness and impartiality, pointing out the discrepancies in the evidence, and recommending the Jury to give the prisoner the benefit of any rational doubt they might entertain.

The Jury retired for five minutes, and then brought in a verdict of NOT GUILTY.

TUESDAY, July 31.

WM. MIDDLETON was convicted of an assault on Edward Williams, at Felling Colliery, on the 1st of July. —To be imprisoned 12 calendar months, and to enter into his own recognizance for his good behaviour for 2 years.

THOMAS EDDY, aged 20, HENRY DINNING, aged 23, JAMES GREY, aged 24, CHARLES STEPHENSON, aged 20, and WM. BELL, aged 16, were indicted for a riot and assault in the parish of Jarrow, on the 15th May last. The prosecutor, Joseph Lilburn, with some other boys, was leaving work at Manor Wallsend Colliery, about 4 o'clock in the afternoon. When they came near to South Shields, a crowd of persons were standing, among whom were the prisoners. Grey threw Lilburn down, and he was severely beaten. Dinning was not seen to strike at the prosecutor.—The prisoners were indicted for cutting and maiming Lilburn, but he not having appeared, the prisoners were tried on the counts for the riot and assault. Dinning acquitted; the others guilty of the assault. —Each to be imprisoned 1 year, and to enter into their own recognizances for their good behaviour for 2 years.

RIOT AT FRIAR'S GOOSE.

THOMAS ARTHUR, aged 22, WILLIAM WESTGARTH, aged 23, JOHN BARKUS, aged 46, WILLIAM CARR, aged 25, GEORGE DURHAM, aged 20, STEPHEN CROZIER, aged 23, ADAM GUTHRIE, aged 17, ABIGAIL MOUTER, aged 27, WILLIAM NOBLE, aged 37, JAMES NICHOLS, aged 46, JOHN WORLEY, aged 19, JOHN ANDERSON, aged 27, EDWARD BUCHAN, aged 17, WILLIAM HALL, aged 20, ELIZABETH LAING, aged 50, and JOHN MOUTER, aged 30, were indicted for a riot and assault at Friar's Goose Colliery, on the 4th of May. The owners of the colliery had procured a number of constables, under Mr Forsyth, from Newcastle, to assist in expelling the pitmen from their houses. When they commenced their operation, a great crowd gathered together and hissed and abused them. The first house that was entered was occupied by Thomas Carr, who requested that his furniture might be carried to Gateshead. When the carts with the furniture were set on to the road, a number of people followed. After they had got a short distance on the road, the constables were attacked, and their arms were taken from them. Shortly after a general riot ensued, and many stones were thrown, and some of the constables much hurt, and they were obliged to fire to defend themselves, and make good their retreat.—Some of the arms were deposited in the guard house, which were taken away by the mob, and the man who had them in charge was roughly handled. Barkus, W. Carr, Durham, Laing, and J. Mouter, were in the mob at the houses in the morning, but were not seen in the riot which ensued afterwards. Worley, Noble, Nichols, Arthur, Guthrie, Anderson, Hall, Buchan, Crozier, and A. Mouter, were recognized in the mob where the police were attacked, but were not all observed to do any thing amiss.—Noble, Nichols, Arthur, Anderson, Buchan, Crozier, A. Mouter, and Barkus, were found guilty, and the rest acquitted.—Anderson to be imprisoned 21 calendar months, Arthur 18 calendar months, Buchan and Crozier each 15 calendar months, A. Mouter and Barkus, each 1 year, and 9 calendar months to hard labour, and each to enter into his own recognizance for good behaviour for 2 years.

WEDNESDAY, August 1.

MURDER OF MR FAIRLES.

At the sitting of the Court this morning, WILLIAM JOBLING, aged 30, was arraigned for the murder of the late Mr Fairles, the Magistrate at South Shields, under the circumstances described in the public prints at the period of the transaction. The prisoner was dressed in a blue jacket, black trowsers, yellow striped waistcoat, and black cravat. He appeared much dejected. The indictment charged James Armstrong (who has absconded) with committing the murder, by beating the head of the deceased with a stone, and Jobling with aiding and abetting him therein. The prisoner was also charged with the offence on the Coroner's Inquest. He pleaded not guilty; and after two challenges on the part of the prisoner, and one for the Crown, the Jury were impannelled.

Mr Coltman and Mr Ingham conducted the prosecution, and Mr Archbold appeared for the prisoner.

The prisoner having been given in charge,

Mr Coltman, in opening the case, said the Jury had heard the nature of the charge against the prisoner, which was the highest in point of guilt known to the law. He entreated them to give the case the most vigilant and impartial attention, because it was important, on the one hand, that high crimes should not go unpunished, and, on the other hand, that persons charged with their perpetration should have the protection of that caution which it behoved juries to exercise in the administration of justice. The learned gentleman said Mr

Fairles, at the time he received the outrage which occasioned his death, was proceeding from South Shields, towards Jarrow Colliery, where he had taken up his temporary residence, for the purpose of superintending the measures that were taken against the pitmen at that colliery. That he was foully murdered by some person or other was beyond all doubt; and the question which the jury would have to decide would be whether the prisoner was identified with the transaction. The learned gentleman then proceeded to state the facts of the case, which he related with great temper and moderation.

Mr INGHAM then called

Mr John Arthur Forster, who said, I am the viewer at Jarrow Colliery, which is two miles from South Shields. I made a plan of the road, which is a raised causeway. [The plan was put in.] On Monday, the 11th of June, I was passing from South Shields to Jarrow. It was about four o'clock in the afternoon. The prisoner, who is a pitman, belonged to our colliery. I saw him on my way home, near to the Turnpike Gate. He was on the Shields side of the gate when he first came up to me. He was coming in the direction from Turner's public house. He asked me for something to drink; but I did not give him any thing. I then saw Ralph Armstrong, whom I had known before, coming running towards me in the same direction that Jobling had come. On seeing him coming I gave Jobling a shilling, and as soon as he left hold of my bridle rein I went off to Jarrow. Jobling took hold of the reins of my horse—he took his hat off and accosted me civilly. He went towards Turner's public house. I did not see what direction Armstrong took. I knew Mr Fairles, who was to stay, that night, at my house, in Jarrow. He was called upon to stay at Jarrow, as a magistrate, through fear of mischief arising at the colliery. He had been at my house from the 30th of May, or longer. Armstrong and Jobling had been working with us previous to the last strike, but not after that.

Cross-examined.—Jobl ng accosted me civilly, but I had no doubt when he took my bridle he intended to stop me. He asked me civilly for something to drink, as his old master, and laid his hand on my bridle, and that I call stopping.

By the JUDGE.—I was going to Jarrow.

Mary Taylor.—I live in North Shields. On the 11th o June I was along the road leading to South Shields. I was going towards that place from Jarrow. The first thing I saw was a pony shaking its head up. It was about half past five o'clock in the afternoon. There is a turn in the road. I was coming towards the toll-gate. I walked on, after seeing the pony; and soon I heard a cry of "Murder." I still went on, and before I got round the turn I saw a man's feet in the air above the wall. I ran till I got round the turn. I heard the cry of "murder" first, and afterwards saw the feet in the air. When I saw the feet in the air, the pony was wide of the feet, and had come towards me. When I ran round the corner, I saw three men struggling on the ground: they were all three down, scuffling, one over each other. I made up as fast to them as I could. My aunt was with me, and she cried out, "You murdering villains, you are murdering the man." Two of the men then looked round and ran off. I went up and found Mr Fairles lying on the ground. When my aunt cried out, one of the men was holding Mr Fairles down and the other was striking him. I did not hear either of them say any thing. The man was striking Mr Fairles with a large thick white stick, with the appearance of no bark upon it. The man who was striking him was leaning double, and the man who was holding Mr Fairles down was on the ground. On my aunt calling out, the man dropped the stick after striking Mr Fairles again; the other got up, and they both ran away towards South Shields. The man who was holding Mr Fairles had a blue jacket and blue trowsers on: the other had a dark coloured dress on; he had a coat on, which was dark coloured. Mr Fairles got up when I got to him; and I led him to Mrs Blenkinsop's gate. My daughter (Mary Pusey) was with me, besides my aunt (Margaret Hall). Before I got to Mrs B.'s gate, I met her servant. She led Mr F., to the gate, and I parted from him there.

Mr Robb, police officer at Shields, produced the stick. It was a white horn stick which Mr F. used to carry. It was much smeared with blood at the thick end; and the witness (Mary Taylor) on recognizing it, said it was much more so at first.

Margaret Hall.—I am the aunt of the last witness, Mrs Taylor. I had been at Jarrow, and was returning with my niece and her daughter towards Shields. When I got to the bridge on Jarrow Slake, I heard a noise as if some persons were quarrelling. I did not see who it came from as there was a bend in the road. I saw a pony's head coming towards us, and I ran on, when I saw a person's feet going up as if they were heaving him off the pony. I continued to go on, and when I got in sight of the people, I saw three men, one of whom was lying on the ground, and the other were beating him. I cried "You murdering villains, you are murdering the man." I heard Mr Fairles cry "Murder" several times, and heard one of the men say "Kill him, kill him." One of them was beating him with a stick, and the other was saying, "Kill him, kill him." When we got up to Mr Fairles the other men had gone off. We had got within twenty or thirty yards when they ran off, towards Shields. I lost sight of them when they passed the turn before coming to the turnpike gate. [The witness here corroborated the evidence of Mrs Taylor as to the dresses of the men.] I made no remark as to the persons of the men. Mr Fairles got up by himself, and some other persons, whom I don't know, came and joined us. We left him at Mrs Blenkinsop's gate.

Cross-examined.—Blue jacket and trowsers are very common in that part of the country.

Mary Pusey, a little girl, was next sworn; but as it appeared she could only depose to the same facts, she was not examined.

Robert Stewart.—I was in Turner's public house on the afternoon of the 11th of June. Jobling, Armstrong, and some others were there. Jobling had some money, but I cannot tell where he got it. We had something to drink there: he said he had got it from Mr Forster: it was a shilling. It was laid on the table and spent. After that had been done, Mr Fairles, on a pony, passed the house, going towards Jarrow. I was standing beside the door, and Jobling was standing there too. He said, "There's Mr Fairles; I'll go and ask him for something to drink." I saw him go up to Mr Fairles, and walk alongside the pony. Armstrong was at the public house; but I cannot say whether in the house or at the door. After Mr Fairles passed, Armstrong went towards Shields as far as the end of the row of houses, when he turned, and went along the road the other way, towards Jarrow. I saw Mr Fairles and Jobling through the gate; and Armstrong also, but they were out of sight when Armstrong went through. I saw him till he was out of sight, going the same direction. I saw Jobling and Armstrong again in a quarter of an hour or 20 minutes. I was then playing at quoits at the public house door. They were running, and were near together—nearly breast for breast. They kept right along the road, past the public house. I could see towards Shields some distance; but I took no further notice. I cannot say how Jobling was dressed. Armstrong had a coat on.

Cross-examined.—I have known Jobling for twenty years. Since I first knew him I have been a long time from the colliery: but I have been there for a year, and he bore a very good character for humanity and good conduct as far as I know.

Esther Doran.—I live on Jarrow Slake, next to Turner's public house—nearer to the Turnpike Gate than Turner's. On this afternoon I saw Jobling speak to Mr Forster. I saw Mr Fairles pass afterwards. I was at the door. It was between 5 and 6 o'clock. I saw Jobling go up to him and ask for something to drink. Mr Fairles replied he thought he stood no need of it, and Jobling said he knew better—he did. They passed on through the Turnpike Gate together. I saw Armstrong go on after that: he was running after them. I saw them 10 minutes or a quarter of an hour after that, running back together, very fast, in the direction of Templetown, the extremity of Shields. I observed that Armstrong's hands were all blood on the back. I was not at the door all the time between their going and coming back. After I saw these men pass, I saw Mr Fairles come along all blood: he was then coming to the Toll Gate, and then he went towards Mr Blenkinsop's.

Cross-examined.—The prisoner was talking with Mr Fairles as they passed my door; and they were conversing in a particularly friendly way as far as I saw. I did not hear the prisoner say "Ah hinny, Mr Fairles, you'll give me another sixpence—'tis not the first one." I have known the prisoner about a year; but know nothing about his character for humanity.

Bridget Davison.—I live servant with Mr Bell in South Shields. I was at my sister's house, the next door to Turner's, on the 11th of June, when this happened. I saw Mr Fairles riding past on a pony, towards Jarrow, about five o'clock. A man, who was said to be Jobling, was going alongside of him with his hand on the pony's back. I don't know it was the prisoner; and I did not hear him say any thing. I saw them go through the Turnpike Gate together. I did not remark how he was dressed. There was a man going towards Shields, who stopped at the end of the row and turned again. I heard him say, but without speaking to any body, "Let us kill him;" and then he put his hand under his coat. I don't know that man; but he was dressed in a black coat. The other man, who went with Mr Fairles, was out of hearing at that time. After the man turned back, he went straight on through the Toll Gate. I cannot tell how far he was behind Mr Fairles and the other man at that time. I saw the two men again in about ten minutes or a quarter of an hour. They both ran past my sister's house towards Shields. The tall man's hands were all bloody. That was the man in the coat, who said "Let's kill him." I heard the tall man say, in passing, "We'll run straight on." I was in the road when I heard that expression; and standing in the window, which was open, when I heard the man use the first expression. After I saw these men returning, I went through the turnpike, and met Mr Fairles, Mrs Blenkinsop's servant, and three other women. Mr F.'s head was all bloody. He went to Mrs Blenkinsop's. I saw the stick. Mr F. had his hat and stick in his hand at the time. He let the stick fall, and said "My dear, will you pick my stick up?" and I did. [The stick was shewn.] That is the stick. It was bloody at the time. I saw a large wound on the left side of Mr Fairles' head.

Cross-examined.—There is a wall opposite to my sister's house.

Re-examined.—That is on the side of the road opposite.

By the Judge.—I gave that stick to the constable.

By Mr Archbold.—There are not fields at the other side of that wall: it is Jarrow Slake; which, at high water, is flooded, and at low water muddy.

Re-examined.—It is a raised road, and my sister's house is on the land side.

John Hinde.—I was in the Toll-house between 5 and 6 in the afternoon, and saw Mr Fairles and his pony go through the gate, and a man walking by his side. I did not see how the man was dressed. The man was asking for a quart of ale, and Mr F. said he would have given him one if he had been sober. They went on together till they were out of sight.—In a few minutes, I saw another man with a coat on, running, with his hand under his coat, in the direction Mr Fairles had gone. I shortly after saw two men running back towards Shields, but observed nothing particular about them, as I was within the door then. In about a minute, I heard a cry that Mr Fairles was murdered. I went out and met Mr Fairles coming towards Mrs Blenkinsop's, about 180 yards from the gate. His left eye was much cut; there was a cut over the right one also, and there was some blood on his head.

By Mr Archbold.—Did not Mr Fairles tell you that Jobling did not touch him?

Witness.—He said he did not. At Mr Blenkinsop's, when leaning over a chair, and speaking to himself, he said, "Oh, Jobling, Jobling, if you had helped me, when I had him down, I would have mastered him."

Re-examined.—He said Jobling was one, but did not hurt him. When we got to Mrs Blenkinsop's house, I asked him if he knew the men? He said he knew Jobling, but he did not touch him.

By the Judge.—He said "touch him," to the best of my knowledge.

By Mr Coltman.—He said Jobling came to him near to the Turnpike Gate, called him his friend, and asked him for a quart of ale; and when he found he would not give him one, he asked him to shake hands with him, and while they were shaking hands another person came in behind him and pulled him back off his horse; but Jobling never hurt him; though he did not prevent the other from doing so. Then he asked for pen and paper, and wrote a few lines (which witness produced.)

Mr ARCHBOLD objected that the writing was not evidence.

Mr Justice PARKE sustained the objection.

By Mr ARCHBOLD.—It was after that he leant over the chair and said "Jobling, Jobling," &c.

Isabella Robson.—I am servant with Mrs Blenkinsop, whose house is a very little distance from the toll bar. On the evening of this day, I heard an alarm of Mr Fairles's being ill used, which brought me down to the Slake. On going down I met Jobling and another man running towards the toll-bar. One of them said, "We've finished the old b——r." I cannot tell which said it; but they were very near—by the side of each other. One of the men's hands were bloody; but I don't remember which. I went on about 50 yards when I met Mr Fairles, and then I went with him to Mrs Blenkinsop's. He was not in sight when the men passed. I gave the stick to the officer.

Elizabeth Gray.—On the afternoon this happened, I was at Mr Harrison's public house, the Plough, which is nearer to Shields than Turner's. I saw two men come along. One of them was Armstrong; but I don't know who the other was; he was so much in liquor I could not see his face. They were coming sharply along, between a run and a walk, in the direction from Turner's. Armstrong waved his hand to me, and it was all over blood. They *persevered* past the Plough, one after the other, on the way to Shields. Armstrong had a blue coat on; and the other a jacket of a darkish colour.

Mr Robb, captain of the police at Shields, said he apprehended Jobling on the race course, on the Sands, at Shields, about two and a half hours after the outrage. He was dressed in a dark jacket and trowsers. I don't know what state they were in, they were so much tewed in his attempting to escape.

Cross-examined.—The Sands was quite a public place, many other persons being present at the races.

Mr Wm. Eddowes, surgeon, at South Shields, said,—I was called in to Mr Fairles. I saw him between 5 and 6 o'clock. I found him sitting on a chair, bleeding freely from the nose into a basin he held on his knee. He had a wound on the right of the scalp about four inches long, and another over the left eye, about three inches long. His skull was fractured; and there was a fissure large enough to see the brain through it. He was perfectly collected in his mind. He was removed to his own house the same evening. I attended him till he died, on the 21st. I examined his head after his death. The bone of the superior orbit of the left eye was fractured, and two or three portions of the bone driven through the membrane into the brain. I have seen the stick. The fracture was a wound such as a stick like that, a brick, or a stone, would produce. The wounds I have described, and the inflammation they produced, were undoubtedly the cause of the death.

The deposition of Mr Fairles, sworn to before Mr Loraine, the Magistrate, in presence of the prisoner, was put in and proved by Mr Cockerill, the Magistrates' Clerk at Shields. It was as follows :—

He said, that about five o'clock in the afternoon he was proceeding on his pony from South Shields to Jarrow Colliery; and after he had passed Turner's public house he was followed by a man, who, after he had got some yards through the Toll Gate, came up, took hold of his pony, and asked him to treat him with a quart of ale. He said he would not, as he appeared to have had sufficient. The man said, " Do; for I love you as I love my own father." He asked him his name, and he said it was Jobling. He told the man he was afraid the Pitmen had been led away. At that moment, he felt some other person pulling at the cape of his great coat. He had hardly time to turn round till they pulled him from his pony, and the other man said " We will now do for you, you old b——r." He struggled with Jobling, who got upon him and held him down with his arms and knees; and one of them said,—but he could not recollect which,—" We will finish you." The other man struck him several blows with a stone, while Jobling held him down under the pony. When he felt the blows with the stone, he asked if they were going to murder him. He then heard some women calling out, and the two men got up and ran away, he believed in the direction of Shields. He added, that when Jobling first accosted him he asked him (deceased) if he knew him, and he said he did, and that if he thought he had stood in need of a quart of ale, he would perhaps have given him one. After this conversation the other man came up. He believed his name was Armstrong, who had been a Pitman at Jarrow Colliery. The deposition concluded by stating that the prisoner was the man named Jobling who held him down.

The answer which the prisoner made to it was, that he never did Mr Fairles any harm—that he never *mis-lested* him.

Thos. Elstob, whose name was on the back of the indictment, but who was not called in support of the prosecution, was put into the box at the request of Mr Archbold, and examined by him as follows :—I was at Turner's public house on this day. The prisoner was playing at quoits outside the door, along with Stewart. Armstrong was in the public house: he came out and went down the road towards Shields. I saw him come back in about 10 minutes. I know the prisoner. I cannot say what character he bears in point of courage: he is not fond of fighting; he is notoriously a great coward. If he saw any one struggling or quarrelling I think he would scamper off and not stay to assist either party.

This closed the case for the prosecution.

Mr Justice Parke :—Prisoner,—You have heard the charge against you, and the evidence in support of that charge; and now is the time for you to address to the Jury any thing you may have to say in answer to it. You will understand that your Counsel is not at liberty to speak for you, and can only examine your witnesses.

The prisoner said,—I am innocent of the charge. When I was talking to Mr Fairles, Armstrong came and pulled him off his horse. I ran away, seven yards, I think; when I shouted back to him to behave and let him alone. I ran away then nearly as far as the turnpike gate; and then I looked back and saw Armstrong standing *striddle-legs* across him, and another man, not Mr Fairles, standing beside him. I had not got far through the turnpike gate when Armstrong overtook me and said "Run;" and I ran off with him.

Mr Archbold then called

James Boag Hancock, —— Fowler, Robert Woodruff, John Rankin, Thomas Atty, Peter Bulmer, James Stanley, George Peel, pitmen, and Joseph Liddell, a mechanic, who said they had known the prisoner for several years, and gave him a good character for peaceable conduct and humanity.

The learned Judge then summed up the evidence at length. The points the Jury would have to decide were, whether the prisoner was present at the outrage—next, whether he was there voluntarily—and then, whether he assisted in the commission of the violence which led to the fatal result.

The Jury, after being absent a quarter of an hour, returned a verdict of GUILTY.

When the prisoner was asked what he had to say why sentence of death should not be pronounced against him, he replied, "I am innocent of the crime."

Mr Justice Parke, after placing the awful emblem of justice on his head, addressed the prisoner as follows:—William Jobling,—The Jury who have just pronounced their verdict against you have performed a painful duty to their country under the solemn obligation of their oath. It remains for me to perform mine, a duty as painful; and to tell you that for this offence, of which you have been most properly convicted, the law of your country says you shall die. It has been proved against you by evidence so clear as not to leave any reasonable doubt in the minds of the Jury—or I am sure they would have availed themselves of it; and I believe it has left no reasonable doubt in the mind of any person who has witnessed the trial of the case, and attended to the evidence, that you were guilty of assisting that other wicked man who actually committed this atrocious murder. You said you were present, but did not assist him, and that he was assisted by another man in perpetrating the murder. That account has been disbelieved: it was impossible to credit it. Even by your own account you have been guilty of a want of moral principle which, I trust, is seldom found to exist in this country. The proof against you, on the evidence of Mr Fairles, is so clear and decisive, that there can be no doubt of your guilt. I am afraid this is one of the melancholy consequences of that combination amongst workmen which has prevailed in this county for so long a time—and of which we have witnessed many while sitting here; combinations which are alike injurious to the public interests, and to the interests of those persons who are concerned in them. To that cause I attribute that want of moral principle which could induce you to stand by and assist a person in inflicting a mortal blow on that Magistrate, who appeared to have been actively employed at that time. It is impossible to hold out to you any hope of mercy in this world. Your crime is so heinous, even supposing you did not originally concur in advising Armstrong to commit the fatal act, nor join him in planning it, but only acted with him at the moment of its actual performance, that your life cannot be spared. As surely as the sun shall rise, the day after tomorrow, you will suffer an ignominious death on the scaffold;

and I trust in God that death will operate as it is intended to do—as a warning to all others, and deter them from following the example of your crime. I implore you to make the most of the short interval you will be permitted to remain here in fervent supplications to the throne of grace: your only hope is in the employment of your time in deep contrition, and in imploring the divine pardon, through the merits of our great Mediator. I must now proceed to pass on you the sentence of the law; and I am bound, by that law, as it exists at this moment, to adjudge that your body, after death, shall be hung in chains. I trust the sight of that will have some effect upon those who, to a certain extent, are your companions in guilt,—that your companions in those illegal proceedings which have disgraced the county may take warning by your fate. I do not know but that a Bill that has been before Parliament, and which may, by this time, have received the Royal assent, has not taken from me the power to order your body to be dissected; and therefore I must pass such a sentence as shall not be erroneous.—His Lordship then pronounced sentence of death upon the prisoner in the usual terms, ordering his body to be hung in chains, according to the provisions of the Statute in such case made and provided; and concluded by praying that the Almighty might have mercy on his soul!

The prisoner heard the verdict and sentence without any apparent emotion, and retired from the dock, muttering, we understand, "The Lord preserve you from such as this!"

THE MURDER AT HETTON.

JOHN TURNBULL, aged 39, was indicted for the wilful murder of John Errington, at Hetton Colliery, by shooting him with a gun, on the 21st of April last, and GEORGE STRONG, aged 28, LUKE HUTTON, aged 26, and JOHN MOORE, aged 21, were charged with aiding, counselling, and abetting him therein. They were also arraigned on the Coroner's Inquest. They severally pleaded "Not Guilty."

Mr WILLIAMS observed that after what had been said in the former enquiry, he would not waste time by entering into any observations upon the character of the present case. It was necessary, however, that he should lay before the Jury, in order to their proper understanding of the subject, an outline of the circumstances connected with the late strike. Having done this, and detailed the facts which he said would be proved in evidence,

Mr INGHAM called

Susan Errington, who said, my husband was a pitman at Hetton. He was bound on the 10th of April. He belonged to the Pitmen's Union last year; but not this year. When he bound himself it was like leaving the Union. Our house was in Easington lane, near to the Brick-garth. A great many of our neighbours were off work; and a few chance ones were bound. On the night of the 21st of April, my husband was brought in by some soldiers. He was rather taken in liquor, but not a great deal. He remained in the house about five minutes, and then went out, saying he would go for a short time, and I never saw him again alive. In about eight or ten minutes after he had left I heard the report of a gun; and in a quarter of an hour after that other two were discharged, nearly together—the hindmost seemed heaviest of the two. I know Strong. He lived next door to us. He was not a bound man. On the Thursday he abused my husband about his binding, but it was nothing of importance. On the Friday morning I heard a firing from near Strong's door,—a gun was fired three or four times. I did not see who did it, but my step-mother did. On the same day our boys were playing together, and he came and took his boy, saying " Come away —I don't allow you to play here." He looked at me. He came back and said, " You may all bar your doors and windows—they're coming to put us out of our houses, and the game's just going to begin." He then clapped his hand upon his breeches, and said " We'll have money in our pockets when the black-legs have none." Those who are not bound give that name to the bound men.

Cross-examined by Mr BLACKBURN.—Some men were put out of their houses on Saturday, with the whole of their furniture, which they had to watch. When my husband went out, I don't know whether he went to the house of a person named Holt. I don't know the distance of the place where he was found from Mrs Smith's public house. Both the latter shots I heard seemed to come from the same direction. I was not aware of my husband having any quarrel with Holt. Next day I said Holt had done the deed; but that was because some women told me he had been found out.

Elizabeth Holt.—I saw the deceased on Saturday the 21st April. He left our house in company with Wm. Steele, his son Scott Steele, and John Epplethwaite. I heard the report of a gun about five minutes after he left our house. I heard the report of two guns, but one was a great deal louder than the other, and very near each other; there was not a minute between them. Errington had a pistol when he came to our house, which he loaded there with some powder and shot.

Cross-examined.—When Wm. Steele went out he had a gun; but I did not mind that his son had one. Epplethwaite had no arms. I was in the house when I heard the gun. I thought the two reports proceeded from the same place.

By Mr WILLIAMS.—The sounds seemed to come down the road that the man had gone. There is a place called the Front Street in the Brick-garth, leading from our house to Easington-lane. The report proceeded from that street.

William Steele.—I live in the Brick-garth. I was a bound man on the 21st of April. I became such on the 16th. I had belonged to the Union a little before. I have been a soldier formerly. Before the 21st, I had been entrusted with a gun, a pistol, some powder, 40 rounds of ball, and

20 cartridges of large shot. The storekeeper of the Hetton Colliery, Mr Stark, gave me them. I gave my son the pistol, which I loaded for him. I was to go round, as a constable, between Holt's house and my own. We were two bound men. On this Saturday, I went into Holt's house, in the square, about half past eleven at night. My son and Epplethwaite went in with me; and Errington was there when we arrived. He was a little in liquor. He had a small pistol, which he took from his waistcoat pocket and loaded with powder and shot. When he loaded her, the cock was in the pan. I went out with him and my son.

By the JUDGE.—I asked him why he had not primed it, and he gave me a reason.

By Mr WILLIAMS.—I went out with Errington and my son. He asked me to set him home. When we got out, Epplethwaite joined us. I and Errington proceeded along the front street, on his way home. I desired my son and Epplethwaite to go behind a bush on the other side of the street from my house, and remain there in concealment; and I particularly desired my son to keep an eye upon me till I returned. I know where Robt. Anderson lives, and where a fire was lighted by Cowey, who had been turned out of his house, near to his furniture. I observed that fire about 10 o'clock that night, and not before. I was not at it, and did not know any thing as to who was about it till I took Errington up the street. I took him on his way home about 50 or 60 yards from Holt, the constable's house, and near about a hundred from Cowey's fire. I stopped opposite widow Addison's door. I remained there, in a triangular direction, so that when the deceased left me my eyes were partly upon him. That was on a rising ground. I did not go on because I dared not. He did go on; and I saw him past the fire. He was easy to know, as he was a cripple, and greatly affected in his walk. When he passed the fire I directly lost sight of him. He went homeward. I heard the discharge of a musket in a minute, or a minute and a half after, which seemed to come from Cowey's fire. It was in one report, and was a tremendous large one—I could tell no pause. After I heard that report, my son and Epplethwaite flew up to me. They had been stationed about 50 yards behind me. We all three returned back into concealment beside the bush. We did not see any of the prisoners. I went home, with my son and Epplethwaite, about ten minutes past 12, and I think the heavy report was about 10 minutes before that. In the morning, about 3 o'clock, I went with the picquet to Anderson's house. About 2 o'clock Holt and Epplethwaite went to the Station House for the picquet. I had been in my house from going in to the time they went for the picquet. I did not fire my gun at the time that report was made; and did not see the deceased again alive.

Cross-examined.—I was dressed in a blue jacket and blue trowsers. My house and Holt's are near each other.—

Errington's house is a good way from Holt's. (It is 400 or 500 yards.) He was in Holt's when I went in. He took his pistol out and loaded it in Holt's house. I went a certain distance with him, and durst not go further. I don't know what use the pistol would be of to him without being primed. I know the place where Cowey's fire was, and where the body was found. I know Mrs Smith's public house; and between that and the spot where the body was found I believe there is an unfinished building, but I cannot say. Between Cowey's fire and Anderson's house there is a passage runs along from an oven. I think it will be about two yards from Cowey's fire. I did not observe another fire at Atkinson's. I heard several guns go off that night from the same quarter. A good many people might be about the fire; but I don't know. I never was taken up and examined on this charge. I went forward and gave evidence before the Magistrates on the second day. Nobody ever charged me with this; and I never heard of it till Mr Maynard, the Coroner, told me Turnbull said he would swear it against me. I know the public house at Elemore Vale. I don't know Robert Forster. Holt did not then charge me with having shot the deceased. Holt and I were at the public house together, but he did not charge me with that. A viewer did not say to me "the less you say about that the better." I did not see the deceased after he passed the fire.

Re-examined.—I did not hear any report of fire arms after that heavy report that night.

By the JUDGE.—His reason for not priming the pistol was he did not want to prime it—he did not want to hurt them, only to flay (frighten) them.

Scott Steele.—I am a son of the last witness. I saw the deceased in George Holt's house at half past 11 o'clock. I left the house with Errington, in company with my father and Errington, and no other person. Epplethwaite was standing at the door and went with us. We went about 30 yards up the Front Street in the direction of Errington's house. Errington went with my father, and we stood in the place where they left us. My father went with Errington about 30 yards, and then Errington went up towards the fire. I saw him pass it. My father was standing upon a hill, in the Front Street, on the opposite side from the fire. It might be 100 yards from the fire where my father stood. I could not see my father distinctly during that time, but he was talking to me to keep my eye on him. After Errington passed the fire, about a minute or a minute and a half, I heard the report of a gun. If there was only one gun fired it must have been tremendously heavy loaden. As Errington passed the fire, I heard a noise like a groan from human voices. After Errington passed the fire, and I had heard the gun, I ran up to my father, who was standing at widow Allison's door. I am quite certain my father did not fire his gun at that time.

John Epplethwaite, a prisoner in custody for leaving his work, said I was out on the Saturday night. Our party had a gun and a pistol. I had a sword given to me by Wm. Steele. I had not seen Errington till I saw him at Holt's. I went out with him. We went about thirty yards up the road with him. Scott Steele and I stood there, and Wm. Steele went further up. Errington went up the front street, and I saw him pass the fire. Wm. Steele went up about Sally Addison's door and stood *fornenst* the door, watching him as far as he could see him. I could see Wm. Steele there. After I lost sight of Errington I heard a very heavy report, but I cannot say whether it was from one or two guns. We went up to Wm. Steele in a minute or minute and half. He did not fire his piece when I heard that report. I heard no other report after that, and I was up all night, along with George Holt, and partly with some soldiers. I had heard some reports that night before,—perhaps ten or a dozen. The heaviest I heard was that when Errington passed the fire. After we joined Wm. Steele, after the report, we went a few times round upon the road, and then we went to Holt's. I know Anderson's house. I was there after the heavy report. We went past the house before the body was taken up. George Holt and I went past. That might be about three or four o'clock in the morning. This was before we saw the soldiers, and after we left Steele. We were going upon a round, and as I went by Anderson's with Holt I thought I saw a man lying. We did not stop because we durst not. The soldiers were at the Colliery; and we went down as soon as we saw the man. We did not see who or what the man was. We came back with two soldiers—Rampling and Potter—to where the man was lying, whom we found to be John Errington, dead. He was lying in the gutter, at George Anderson's house end. He was taken into Anderson's house, where I sat up with the body. There was a great deal of blood about his breast and in the gutter. I saw no blood any where else, though I looked. When I took him up he was warm under the arm-pit; but I did not feel him otherwise. I found a pistol lying by his side in the gutter. It was not day-light then. The pistol was charged, but there was no powder in the pan, and the cock was down. I unloaded it: it was loaded with small shot and powder.

Cross-examined.—I had lodged with Holt some time before. The night before there were some bits of cannon things they were firing below the house where I lived. I had never before heard any thing else fired. When I went with Holt I saw the body lying: he did not. The gutter was half a yard deep. It was lying about a yard from the house corner. His back was lying to the front street ward, and the head was lying towards the opening at the oven.

By the Judge.—When I heard the heavy report, I saw the flash. It flew out of the opening; but I cannot say which opening—it came from the housewards. I speak of the flash from the gun, but cannot say whether it came from the priming or from the mouth of the gun. There are several openings to the eastward beyond Cowey's fire; but I cannot say which it came out of: it came out somewhere about where the body was lying near the fire.

George Holt.—I think I last saw the Steeles and Epplethwaite together about half-past one. As I was going towards Anderson's I saw Cowey sitting with his back to the fire. I saw a man lying in the gutter; but I did not touch the body. I went for the soldiers.

Cross-examined.—I cannot tell at what time Errington, the Steeles, and Epplethwaite left my house, as I was asleep in bed. Cowey was watching the furniture. It would be past two when I went towards Anderson's. I did not see Strong with him. I paid no attention to any other fire than that.

James Rampling, the soldier who took Errington home on the night of the murder. That was about half-past 11 o'clock. As I returned through the Brick-garth I thought I heard the report of fire arms, but could not be sure of it. I saw Epplethwaite again in the morning. He came at 3 o'clock, and we got to the body about a quarter past 3. [The witness deposed to the position of the body, and the carrying of it to Anderson's, to the same effect as Epplethwaite.]

Mr Edger, surgeon, of Hetton, said, I was called in to examine the body of Errington on the Sunday morning, between 7 and 8 o'clock. The principal wound was on the first rib on the left side. There was a hole into his chest, into which I could put my finger. I observed the hole through the waistcoat. I opened the body and found that the course of the wound was directed through the chest. It was caused by a stone marble which had passed directly through the chest, and lodged in the integuments of the back. That wound occasioned his death. The heart was not touched, but it had passed directly through the lungs. There was another hole below, through the waistband, and the folds of his garments, 7 or 8 deep, and I could put my little finger through it, but it only penetrated a little through the skin. I think the two wounds had proceeded from two pieces. If both had come from one piece, and the person firing had been near, the shot could not have spread so much.

Cross-examined.—The lower wound went through the skin. I did not find anything; but I judged it was made by a bullet, or a large shot. It could not be a cut. Both wounds were in front of the body, and in a line.

Mr John Robson.—I am resident viewer at Hetton. I knew the deceased, who was one of our bound men. Out of 12 or 1300 who were bound last year not more than ten persons are bound this year. Turnbull had been in our employment. I saw him on the evening of Monday the 23d, at my house. I was told, by Mr Robert Thompson, he knew something of the circumstance, and I sent for him. Mr Thompson remained at my house. Turnbull stated he had occasion to go out of his house (for a purpose of nature, having a bowel complaint) a little after 12 o'clock. He sat down at the top or south end of the street, at the bottom of which on the west end was Anderson's house. While he was there, he saw a person come past him, with a gun in his hand, a Scotch cap on, and an ordinary man's dress on. The man went down the street, in the direction where Errington was found. He heard the hammer of the gun strike the pan, and saw the flash, but the gun did not go off, as it missed fire. In a quarter of a minute he heard the gun go off. The man then came past him again, and went the way he had come. He (Turnbull) sat still till the footsteps died away, being afraid at the time, and then went home. That man, he would take his oath, was William Steele. I took this down in writing, and after I had taken it down I asked him if it was true, and he said, " Yes, it was." I don't recollect that he stated for what purpose he gave this information. He lived in the opening where Cowey's fire was. He was not then a bound man, but had been in the colliery the year before, up to the 5th April, when the bonds expired. The other prisoners were in the same situation.

Cross-examined.—I don't know how soon he was taken up after that time. I did not see him at large again.—Cowey's fire would be distant from his house 30 or 40 yards. The greater part of the houses belonged to the Hetton Company, but not all of them. Cowey's did. He and a person named Atkinson were turned out the same day. The wages had not been decreased. Some of them were increased on some part of the work. Errington might have gone to Steele's by the back street, where the oven is, instead of the front street; but I don't know that it would be a shorter way. I cannot say how many persons were taken up on this charge.

Robert Cowey.—I am a pitman at Hetton. I ceased to be employed on the 5th of April. On the 21st of April my brother's furniture was lying at the door. A fire was lighted near it; but I don't know when it was lighted. I went to it about 11 o'clock and stopped there till 2 o'clock. A good many others were there during that time. I saw Turnbull, Hutton, and Moore there. I saw Turnbull before I had been a long time there. He had a gun with him. I cannot tell how long he remained there at that time. I think he did not stop long there. I saw him more than once there—I should think 3 or 4 different times.—He had not a gun at each of those times. The second time I saw him he had no gun. That would be near about half past 11. I heard some guns fired that night. I had been only a very short time beside the fire when I heard the first. I only heard one after that. I cannot specify the time I heard the second gun; it might be near about 12.

From the report I judged that came from near Easington lane. I cannot say whether Turnbull was at the fire or not when I heard the second gun. I never saw him with a gun after that.

By the JUDGE.—I saw him at the fire after the first gun was fired, and before the second. He had a gun then. He came to the fire and rested the gun upon the ground. I asked him if that was him who fired the gun—the first one? From being rather hard of hearing, I don't know what answer he made. I believe he went away from the fire before I heard the second shot, because a man desired him to go home with the gun. I saw Errington pass the fire; but I don't remember to have seen him going towards his own house. He went towards Holt's. That would be shortly after I went to the fire. I did not see him return. I did not hear any noise made about the fire—any groaning or marks of disapprobation. I was sitting on the opposite side of the fire from the Front Street. The second report I judged to be a loudish report.

Examination resumed.—I saw Hutton at the fire before 12 o'clock. I don't remember seeing him more than once. I cannot say how long he stopped; but he was there a good bit. I don't recollect his leaving the fire; nor whether it was before or after the second gun. I did not see him have any thing with him. I believe I saw Moore at the fire near about when I went there. I saw him more than once, but cannot say how often. I cannot tell how long he stopped the first time. I believe I saw him there after the second gun was fired. I don't recollect whether he was there when the second gun was fired. I don't remember his leaving the fire the last time. I did not see him have any thing with him.

Cross-examined.—I was sitting watching my brother's furniture. I cannot tell how many persons were at the fire. I don't think there were many women there, but there were some young girls. The persons there were holding mirth one with another. Turnbull had a gun with him, but I did not see any body else have one. Neither Moore nor Hutton had. The witness gave the prisoners a good character for humanity, &c. I did not see a fire at Atcheson's.

Re-examined.—I belong to the Union. So do the prisoners.

By the JUDGE.—After the second shot was fired, I don't recollect Turnbull coming back to the fire; but he was there. He did not, after the second shot, say any thing to me about any man lying dead. But about 1 o'clock he left the fire with another man to go towards Easington Lane. He had been sitting at some fire there; and he and the other man, George Anderson, went towards Easington Lane. He returned again, and then he said he believed there was a man lying dead. He had no gun with him then. That was all that was said. Then two other men went away with him to the same spot.

By Mr DUNDAS.—One of those two men was Thomas Sotheran, and Wm. Wynne, who was taking care of the goods along with me. They took a candle with them; but were not absent above two minutes. They came back and said they thought it was Errington's body. Turnbull asked what was best to be done with it. Sotheran and he went away together; but I don't recollect that they said they were going to a constable.

William Turnbull.—I am no relation of the prisoner. I went to Cowey's fire, but I cannot tell about what hour. I had lodged with William Roseby, and he was turned out. I was at the fire a good while. I saw the prisoner Turnbull there. He was there before I went. George Thornton fired a pistol, and Turnbull fired a gun. I did not observe Tuurnbull with a gun before he fired it, nor with one after. He went away up to the backside of the row directly after he fired, and I did not see him that night again. He went towards Smith's public house, and towards his own house. I saw Strong there. He was at Robert Lawson's house end. He had a gun. I saw him twice that night: he had a gun both times. As I was going up the row, to Atcheson's fire, I heard him threaten very sore. He made me mention my name, and said if it had been Geordy Holt he would have blown his brains out. I went into Atcheson's, and he went in also. Robert Kennett took the gun from him and fired it up in the air. Kelly said to him, do you know what ill you are doing me in that night? I saw Moore at Atcheson's fire. He said there was a man lying with his legs up. I asked where it was, and he replied to me, "Do you want your liver knockep out, you b——r?" He said, also, did I want another Easington touch? That meant this. I was once at Easington races, where there was a riot. I spoke up, and a man came and felled me into the dyke. I asked him if they were going to kill a man at the races? I went before a Justice on that business. I saw Hutton. He came to Cowey's fire while I was there. Other four were with him, but none of those prisoners. They were William Wilson, Robert Reay, William Robson, and Robert Lowrey. They came together down the row. Hutton said, "Mony a time Errington and he had had a fight together, but they would not fight any more, for they had put him by."

Cross-examined.—I cannot tell what time it was when I went to the fire. I went to bed at Matthew Emerson's, but I cannot tell at all what time it was. Edward Nicholson was in bed when I went into the house. It was after 11 o'clock, but I don't know whether it was after 12 or not. It was Emerson's house, but Atcheson had the charge of it. When I went to bed Mary Atcheson was in the house, and she saw me go to bed. There was a camp at Atcheson's also. I went up to it, and Strong was there guarding Atcheson's goods. It was there he had a gun: Henry Nicholson and he had the gun between them. I know Mary Epplethwaite. I was taken up about this matter myself, as well as the others. I was taken to Hetton. I remember the inner room at Hetton. Mary Epplethwaite said "Poor thing what have they handcuffed thee for?" I did not tell her I had laid in bed all that night and knew nothing about it. I was at Durham about 7 weeks. I was not confined in prison, I was only with Mr Frushard. I was brought in on Easter Monday, and stopped till when I went to Hetton again. About 12 of us were handcuffed. I first told the story I have told here to-day a fortnight after that. I had been kept in gaol a fortnight before I told it. I had told part of it to the magistrates at Hetton before I went to gaol. I told them about who had the gun. I told them the first day they took me—that was on the 22d. I work for my living. I am a collier. I had no talk about this matter with Benjamin Embleton. I did not see him on the Sunday. He never asked me where I was on the Saturday night; and I did not tell him I was in bed all the time. I never saw him. I can safely say before my Maker I never told him Holt had done it.

Re-examined.—I don't know Mr Mills, Mr Shipperdson, or Mr Greenwell; but I do Mr Pemberton. I don't remember whether he was one of the Justices that I was before at Hetton on the Sunday. [This witness gave his testimony in a very incoherent manner, and seemed to be a person of weak intellect.]

Mr Frushard, governor of the gaol, said, the last witness came to me on the 23d of April. He was remanded till the 3d of May, for re-examination. He remained with me, at the request of the magistrates, till the 9th June, as it was not considered safe for him to be at large. He then said he was tired of remaining within the walls of a prison, and he would take his chance, and go and get bound to the Hetton owners.

William Winn.—I was living at the Brick-garth, at the time this happened. I had been a Hetton pitman, but was not bound then. I was at Cowey's fire that night. I went about ten o'clock and staid till two. I had been there all that while. Robert Cowey was there. We went home together. Turnbull came to the fire several times, backwards and forwards. He fetched a gun. I heard two guns fired that night. I think it would be after 11 o'clock when the first was fired. I did not see Turnbull there when the first gun was fired. I saw him afterwards. He came from behind the cart, where I was. He stood between the fire and the cart, and set the gun on one end. I heard a second discharge. I saw him resting on the gun before the second report. I did not remark which was the loudest report. At the time of the second report, I did not see Turnbull at the fire. The cart was not far from the fire. The second report appeared to come from Easington Lane-ward. I saw Turnbull again after that. I did not see him come;

but the next I observed of him was, he was sitting smoking his pipe at the fire. He had not a gun then. After that second report, there was another gun fired, high up to the lane-ward. I think that gun would be fired about half-past 12—about half an hour after the second. After seeing Turnbull smoking his pipe, I saw him again. When Harry Nicholson, Robert Kennett (a constable), and Robert Stephenson came, Kennett asked if any body had fired a gun there, and Turnbull said he had fired one. It was after the third shot that Kennett came. When the third shot was fired, Turnbull was smoking his pipe. A man of the name of Sotheran was there. Turnbull and he went away together. Before they went, I did not hear them say what reason they had for going. Before they went away, Turnbull and Anderson walked towards Smith's, saying they would take a walk. They came back and Turnbull said there was a man lying in the gutter. Sotheran then lighted a candle, and Turnbull carried it. I followed them up, and saw a man lying, but I could not see whether he was dead or asleep. That was after Kennett went away. Turnbull and Sotheran returned again to the fire, and said they believed he was shot. Turnbull and Sotheran went up to the body again, and when they came back they said they had turned the body over, and he was shot. They asked what was the best to be done about it; and we said to tell the Police—they were to go away and tell Kennett. They went to the lane; but whether they went to Kennett I don't know. They came back again, and when we asked them what they had done, they said they could get no one to hear them. Kennett's would not be more than a few minutes' walk.. Turnbull went away and I saw no more of him. I don't know any thing of Turnbull's bodily health about that time. I saw Strong that night. I saw him at the fire when I went at 10 o'clock. He had a gun then; but I did not see him again. I saw Moore several times. After the second shot, and before the third, he came to the fire, and said Jack Errington was lying in the gutter watching. He went away the same way he came down—up to the laneward. I saw Hutton at the fire between the first and second shots; but I did not hear him say any thing. The witness Turnbull was at the fire a long time.

Cross-examined.—Several persons were backward and forward as well as the prisoner Turnbull. When Moore said Errington was lying in the gutter, he spoke it aloud, and several other persons might have heard him. [The witness gave the prisoners a good character for humanity and peaceableness.] I don't know that Strong was a watcher at Atcheson's fire that night. I did not know there was a fire.

Re-examined.—I don't know whether any body but Union men were at Cowey's fire that night. I cannot recollect one who was not.

By the Judge.—At the time of the third gun, I cannot

tell whether Robert Cowey was there. I cannot say whether he might hear the third gun.

Robt. Kennett.—I am the constable mentioned by the last witness. I saw Strong on the night of the 21st of April. I saw him a little after twelve at Atcheson's fire. He had nothing with him when I went up; but on looking round I found a gun standing against the pantry or yard-wall. I seized it, and asked the men about the fire who it belonged to. They replied "it is ours." I said what do you mean by saying "ours," and Strong said "ours" again. I took the gun and drew the ramrod, which I put into the barrel to sound it, and found it loaded. I took the gun then, and fired it off at arm's length.

Cross-examined.—Then he gave me his powder flask and I took it away. I knew all the prisoners; but too little to enable me to speak of their character. I was taken up for this affair, and kept in gaol eleven days. Turnbull came to me that morning. Sotheran and he told me they had found Errington lying in the gutter, apparently shot. This was about half-past one o'clock. The reason why I did not go to the place after this was, that men's minds were so much irritated—I was alarmed and my wife was intimidated. I I said I wished he had not come, as I would have to go for the police.

Re-examined.—By the police I meant the London Officers who had been brought down—some soldiers and some police, who were on the patrole. I belong the Union.

Mr Justice Parke.—You may think yourself very lucky you are not indicted, for neglect of your duty.

Mary Epplethwaite.—I am the wife of Wm. Epplethwaite, of Hetton, pitman. On the 21st of that month, we had a gun in our house. It was our own. It had frequently been lent before, to several persons. On the Saturday night Errington was killed, Strong came to our house. My husband was in bed and I was just going. All the family, except my son, were in bed but myself. The door was fastened. He came to it. I was just putting in the bolt when he came. I opened the door; and he asked if I would lend him the gun. It was standing at the bed-foot. This was about 10 o'clock. He got the gun in his hand, and loaded it at the back-house fire side. He put powder in it and paper; but remained no longer than while he did that. I fastened the door and went to bed. I went to sleep. I saw Strong again. He fetched the gun back. He got in at the front door. I was awoke by his lifting the sneck, and I got up and opened the door. By the burning of the fire I thought that might be an hour or an hour and a half after. I asked him if it was loaded, and he said no, Kennett had fired it off and ordered him to take it home. I don't know that it had a flint in when he took it away. He said he wanted it to watch George Atcheson's furniture.

Cross-examined.—I know the witness, Wm. Turnbull. I was in a room at Hetton, when he was brought in handcuffed. I said "Poor thing, where have they had thou?" and he said he had been in bed, and knew nothing about it. Mr Frushard then took him away.

Re-examined.—Mr F. saw him talking with me, and then took him away.

Margaret Bailey.—I live with my husband, John Bailey, in Easington Lane, opposite to Kennett's. I heard 6 guns fired this night, between 10 and 12. The last was exactly at 12. I remarked it from its being so very heavy. The clock had just struck 12. The report seemed to come from the Brick-garth. Anderson's house is in the front Street, in the Brick-garth, and the report came from that direction. On hearing it, I went to my own door-stead, and observed men coming from Kennett's entry in the Brick-garth, across to my door. There were a good many. They were running sharply across the road. I durst not stay longer, and went in and shut the door. I could not make out the persons of any of them—it was so dark.

By the JUDGE.—I know none of the prisoners but Turnbull, and cannot tell whether he was one of those men, or whether they had a gun. There was nothing to prevent them coming from the front street down Kennett's entry. I went to bed, and heard no more reports after that.

Charles Potter, another soldier, said, I was present when the body was found. When it was removed into Anderson's I went back to look for a pistol. I saw it picked up by Epplethwaite. I examined it, and found it was loaded. When the body was taken into the house, there was warmth under the arm-pits, but the hands were quite cold.

This was the case for the prosecution.

Turnbull, on being called upon for his defence, said,—I know nothing of the charge made against me. I am perfectly innocent.

After a considerable pause, occupied by the learned Judge in looking over the depositions in the cause, he requested Winn to be recalled, who, in answer to his Lordship's enquiries, said, that when Turnbull came to the fire and said the deceased was shot, he did not say he had seen Steele fire a gun in that direction. He did not say at all that he saw Steele fire a gun that night.

Robert Cowey said he never heard Turnbull say any thing of the kind either.

Turnbull, on being again called upon by his Lordship, said,—I know no more about it than the child that's unborn.

Strong.—I have nothing to state, but that I'm as clear of it as the child that's in the womb.

Hutton made a similar declaration.

Moore said he knew nothing about it.

Mr BLACKBURN called Robert Watson in behalf of Hutton and Moore, when he was stopped by the Judge, who said there was no case against those prisoners, except the testimony of William Turnbull, on which it did not appear to him the Jury could place much reliance; and the witness was therefore withdrawn.

George Anderson.—I saw Turnbull come to Cowey's fire. He and I went together about half past nine. Turnbull went away almost directly and I remained. Soon after, he came back, behind the camp, with a gun, which he fired. He then set the gun down upon the butt end, and then went away with the gun. I saw no more of him till nearly one o'clock. I went away from the fire into my own house about 12, and about one I returned to the fire, beside Winn and Robert Cowey. After that, he asked me to take a walk to Atcheson's fire. We set off to go. I was behind him, and when he got opposite where the body was, he said "Dear me, here's a man lying." I shrunk back from his saying that word. I retreated to Cowey's fire. He followed me back and said he believed there was a man lying dead. Then Sotheran and he went with a candle. He came back and said it was John Errington, and he was dead. He said that so as the people about might hear him. He asked what was best to be done, and we thought it would be best to send to the constable. He and Sotheran went away for that purpose; and when he came back he went home directly. His house is about 40 or 50 yards from the fire. I have known Turnbull about a year, and live close to him. I know nothing but good of his character for humanity.

Cross-examined.—He fired the gun over the camp about 10 o'clock. I went home to my supper about 12; and while I was there I heard a heavy report, which seemed to come from the north end of the row that I lived in. That was the last report I heard that night. When I returned, I did not see any gun that Turnbull had. I returned to the fire after being about an hour absent. I did not hear how Errington had come by his death, nor mention any body that had done it. I am in the Union.

Thomas Sotheran, a prisoner in the gaol, said,—I went before the Grand Jury yesterday, for the prosecution. I was at Cowey's fire. I went home that way. It would be just about one o'clock when I got there. Turnbull was there when I went. George Anderson was there too. They left the fire together, after I had been there two or three minutes. They returned in two minutes, and said, aloud, that a man was lying. There were not many persons at the fire—only about four. I went with Turnbull with a candle, and either Anderson or Winn followed. We went along to Anderson's house and found a dead body in the ditch. We went back to the fire, and I went with Turnbull to Kennett's. We found him at home, and he was told what had happened. Kennett directed us to say we had not seen him.

Cross-examined.—I am in prison for an assault.

By the Judge.—Turnbull did not mention to me that he had seen Steele fire past Anderson's house.

Henry Nicholson, who was on the back of the indictment, was called by Mr. BLACKBURN. He said,—I was at Atcheson's fire. I saw Strong there. I went about half past 10. He was there when I went. He was watching the goods. I did not see the gun till Robert Kennett came, about 20 minutes past 12. When I left the fire, I left Strong there. I saw Kennett fire off Strong's gun, who gave him the powder flask. I staid at Atcheson's fire half an hour after half past ten, and left Strong there. I went to Cowey's fire, about 250 yards distant. I was a quarter of an hour there, and when I went back to Atcheson's I found Strong there. I continued there till Kennett came, and Strong was there under my eye all the while.

Cross-examined.—There were a goodish few people there whiles, and whiles not so many. I am a Union man. There was one person at Atcheson's-fire who was not a Union man—Thomas Revely. I did not see any body who was not a Union man at Cowey's fire.

John Norsen.—I was at Atcheson's fire this night. I went about 10. I saw Strong there sitting beside the fire. He was just coming when I went to the fire. I staid till between 12 and 1. Strong was there all the time. I did not see him go away for a little, except at the first, when he and I took a walk to the other fire; but we were not more than 10 minutes. About 12 o'clock, when I was at Atcheson's fire, I heard a very loud report. Strong was sitting at the fire at that time. The sound proceeded from the back part of the Brick-garth. It was a heavy report. I remember Kennett coming to Atcheson's fire, about a quarter of an hour after that. He fired Strong's gun off, and got Strong's powder flask. I went away between 12 and 1, about a quarter of an hour after Kennett left. I have known Strong about 12 months. I have never heard any thing bad of him about good nature and humanity.

Cross-examined.—I was a pitman belonging to the Union. Different people were at Atcheson's fire, but I can't tell who they were. Seven and eight were always there. People did not keep going and coming between the two fires. I did not go before the Justices on this matter. I heard of Strong being taken up; but I never was called upon. I don't know any thing about where the Magistrates sat before whom he was examined. I heard of it, but never was down.

Re-examined.—I heard of a good number of other persons being taken before the Magistrates.

Thomas Revely.—I am a corver. I was at Atcheson's fire: I went between 11 and 12. I know Strong by eyesight. He was there when I went. I stopped there till Kennett came. While I was there, I heard a loud report of a gun. It came from the west. At the time I heard that, Strong was standing close by my right hand, and he remained at the fire till Kennett came.

Cross-examined.—Six or eight were there at the time of

the report. During the whole time I was there, persons kept going and coming. I never spoke to Strong before then. The pitmen were in different dresses. I heard of Strong being taken up. I knew of the Justice meeting upon it. It was held at Hetton; and I live at Easington Lane—part of Hetton. I did not go before the Justices—I never was called on.

Re-examined.—Strong had a top coat on.

Benjamin Embleton.—I am a pitman, and reside in the Brick-garth. I know the witness Wm. Turnbull. I saw him on Sunday morning, standing near the house end. I knew him before, and he knew me. I asked him where he was the preceding night. He said he was in bed, and that Holt shot the man.

Cross-examined.—How came you to speak with him? Because I knew he had been turned out. He had not been before the Justices then. I afterwards learnt he was taken up—either on the Sunday evening or Monday morning. I did not go before the Justices, though I knew they were sitting at Hetton. I belong to the Union. I am not a delegate.

Re-examined.—I know of no reason why I should have gone before a Magistrate. I have known Turnbull 7, and Strong 9 years, and they have both had a good character for humanity.

Mary Atkins.—I live in Easington-lane. I know Wm. Turnbull. He slept at my house on the night Errington was killed. He came in, I think about 11, and never went out before he went to bed.

Edward Nicholson.—I lodged with the last witness on the night when Errington was killed. I went in about 11 o'clock. Wm. Turnbull was sitting by the fire when I went in. He slept with me. I went to bed immediately, and he came after me in a minute or a minute and a half.

Cross-examined.—I am in the Union.

Robert Forster.—I am a pitman, and live at Easington Lane. I was at the Elemore Vale public house about 3 weeks after Errington's death. I saw W. Steele and Holt there drinking. I heard Holt say to Steele,—"Drink—you know you shot Jack Errington." There was no viewer there. Jacob Graham, an overman in one of the pits, was there. He said "You had better hold your tongue—the less you say about that the better."

Cross-examined.—Six or eight persons were there. I was not drinking with them; but they spoke loud enough to be heard. Holt was drunk. Steele hung his head and smiled.

Wm. Dent, a schoolmaster, at Easington Lane; Mr Love, a grocer, &c., at Easington Lane; Thomas Coxon, a cabinet maker, at the same place; Thomas Love, an overman in a colliery near North Shields; and Peter Watson, a cordwainer, at Easington Lane, gave Strong a good character for humanity.

Anne Smith, of Easington Lane, and John Coxon, a cabinet maker there, spoke to the same effect in favour of Turnbull.

This was the whole of the evidence.

The learned Judge summed up at great length, and with great clearness and impartiality. The Jury, he said, would acquit Hutton and Moore, for the reason he had already stated, and confine their attention to the cases of Turnbull and Strong. His Lordship dwelt particularly on the statement made by Turnbull to Mr Robson, and left it to the Jury to infer from that fact, and from the circumstance of Turnbull's silence upon the point, on the Saturday night, whether it was a true account, or whether it had been made with a view to conceal his own culpability by fixing the guilt of the transaction upon another, or was fabricated merely in the spirit of wickedness. If the fact had been as the prisoner stated, the Jury would determine how far it was probable that he should refrain from at once charging the offence upon a man obnoxious to him and his companions in the union, to whom that person was obnoxious, and to whom his commission of the crime would, in the nature of things, have been a triumph. They would judge whether his conduct was consistent with guilt or innocence, and find their verdict accordingly. In the course of his Lordship's address, he animadverted strongly on the evident reluctance that there was among the pitmen to disclose the truth. Such a conspiracy to defeat the ends of justice, he said, he could not have believed possible.

The Jury retired for about 5 minutes, and then brought in a verdict of ACQUITTAL, with regard to both prisoners.

This result was not anticipated as to Turnbull; and the announcement evidently created a feeling of surprise amongst the auditory in the body of the court.

JOSEPH YOUNG, aged 21, THOS. COWELL, aged 18, MICHAEL BARKUS, aged 25, JOHN SHOTTON, aged 22, and THOMAS NICHOLS, aged 24, were charged with stealing 5 guns, the property of the Mayor and Corporation of Newcastle, on the 4th of May last. This case arose out of the riot at Friar's Goose Colliery on the 4th of May. William Turnbull, one of the special constables, had been placed to guard the house where the arms were deposited. In the course of the morning, a mob collected round the house, and some of them rushed in and got away the arms, and they also attacked Turnbull and used him very ill. He recognized all the prisoners in the crowd. They were among the first who broke into the house. Another constable, stationed a short distance from the house, saw Shotton come out of the mob with one of the guns. He also saw Cowell and Young in the crowd. Three or four men were seen by another constable to run from the guard house into the crowd, with rifles in their hands, but he could not tell who they were. Mr ARMSTRONG, for the defence, submitted that the offence did not amount to larceny, because the arms were taken merely to disarm the police, and not with any felonious intent. But Mr Baron BOLLAND thought it sufficient to constitute a larceny that the owners of the guns were deprived of their property in them. Witnesses were called to prove that Shotton and Barkus were at their own houses when the guard house was broken open. The learned Baron in summing up left it to the Jury to find whether the offence was a larceny or not.—Acquitted.

NICHOLAS LOWREY, aged 28, WILLIAM THURKELL, aged 34, ROBERT COLE, aged 27, GEORGE DAWSON, aged 33, JOHN AYRE, aged 22, WILLIAM ADDISON, aged 25, and ARCHIBALD DIXON, were indicted for a riot and assault near Pittington, on the 1st of July.—Two of the special constables, John Todd, and Robert Forster, employed at Hetton, who had been at Durham, were on their way home, and fell in with a crowd of persons who were ill using some of the miners who had been employed to work at Hetton Colliery. When the constables got within sight of the mob, a volley of stones was thrown at them, and they were knocked down 2 or 3 times, and much hurt. Some of the miners were also used very ill. Adams, one of the miners, saw Cole at Moody's public house on Gilesgate Moor, and he said to him "You are going to Hetton." Adams replied "That he was not,—he was going to seek mowing." Cole and Dawson were seen in the mob when the stones were thrown. Cole and Dawson were found guilty, and the others acquitted. To be imprisoned to hard labour for one year.

THURSDAY, AUGUST 2.

This morning, ELIZABETH PARKIN, WILLIAM PARKIN (her son), and THOMAS VARTY, who were convicted on Monday, of the capital offence of wounding Thomas Thew, at Sheriff's Hill, with intent to murder or do him some grievous bodily harm, were brought up to receive the judgment of the Court.

Mr Justice PARKE addressed them in a most impressive manner, and in the course of his observations said, that their case was one of the most cruel and brutal ever brought before a Court of Justice. It originated in that fertile source of crime, the combination of pitmen—though the female did not appear to be connected with it, as her husband did not belong to the Union. The prosecutor, when attacked by them, sued for mercy; but instead of granting it they inflicted upon him some cruel and hideous wounds. There could be no doubt they intended to murder him. Their offence were as great, morally, and in the eye of God, as if death had ensued. Looking at the serious nature of the crime, the law declared that the person committing it must die. There could be no doubt that, if death had ensued in this instance, the case would have amounted to one of murder. Considering, therefore, the character of the offence, and regarding the present state of this county, it was his duty to endeavour to prevent others from following their example. Painful as the task was to him, he must pronounce upon them the extreme sentence of the law. The female prisoner had been recommended to mercy by the Jury; and if he found, upon enquiry, that she deserved the character she received on the trial, she might expect a mitigation of her punishment. But to the men he could hold out no hope. He implored them, therefore, to lose no time in availing themselves of the spiritual assistance they would receive in the gaol, in making their peace with the Almighty, before whom they must shortly appear. His Lordship then sentenced the prisoners to be hanged.

The men heard their doom with great firmness and composure; but the woman burst into tears, and declared that she was innocent, and was in bed when the offence was committed.

THE ROBBERY AT HETTON.

ROBERT WELSH, who pleaded guilty of robbing James Napier on Monday, was placed at the bar; and the learned Judge, in addressing him, said that his offence had also arisen from the Union. It was one of great enormity. A little more violence would have been fatal; and in that case the prisoner would have been left for execution. His Lordship said he had given the case much serious consideration; and he had determined to recommend the prisoner to the mercy of the Crown. He must, however, expect to leave the country for the remainder of his life.

SAMUEL BERTRAM, aged 29, was charged with being accessary, with persons unknown, who, on the 19th of May last, at the parish of Washington, fired a gun into the dwelling-house of George Wake, with intent to intimidate him. The prosecutor had come from the neighbourhood of Bishop Auckland to work at Mount Moor Colliery, after the pitmen's strike. The prosecutor lives in the same house with the defendant. On the night in question, when they were in bed, they were disturbed by a dog barking, and heard some pitmen outside ask to have their pipes lit. The defendant got up and gave them a light. Shortly after, some person was heard to shout, "are you not going to begin?" and directly after some guns were fired into the prosecutor's house, and part of the charges entered the wall, about 8 inches above the heads of the persons in bed. For the prosecution it was contended, that the defendant must have known who fired the guns. It was asserted in defence, that the defendant could not tell who fired the guns, because the light was given through the key-hole of the door.

Three witnesses were called, and swore that they heard the door opened, and that a conversation ensued between Bertram and the men outside. His Lordship, in summing up, said that this case arose out of the lamentable system of combination which existed to so alarming an extent in this part of the kingdom; but which, he trusted and believed, was now drawing to a close. He did not believe that in any other part of the kingdom any person would refuse to come forward and give evidence in such a case as this; and it shewed the demoralised state of society to which the Colliers' Union had reduced the country. The Jury must be of opinion, in order to convict the defendant, that he actually knew the men who committed the felony, and not that he had only a suspicion of them.—Guilty. To be imprisoned 12 calendar months.

EXECUTION OF JOBLING.

FRIDAY, August 3.

Jobling was executed this day, upon the Drop in front of the County Courts, pursuant to his sentence, the justice of which he acknowledged after retiring to the prison from his trial. He spent the interval between his sentence and his execution in unremitting prayer; and his conduct, for some weeks previous, had been equally devout and penitent. He was led from his apartment in the Gaol a few minutes after 12 o'clock; and he walked with a firm step to the place of execution. On reaching the Grand Jury Room, he knelt down to pray, and repeated the Lord's prayer, and afterwards uttered a short extempore supplication, both in an audible voice, with very correct emphasis and pronunciation, and much earnestness of manner. After some time spent in devotion with the Chaplain, he resigned himself to the Executioner, by whom he was pinioned. At this moment, he desired that some papers which he carried in his pocket might be thrown amongst the crowd; but on being told there would be no persons near the scaffold, he requested that they might be given to a man named Peter Bulmer, of Shields. He was then led out upon the drop, which he mounted with extraordinary steadiness. He took his neckcloth off himself, and looked anxiously round upon the spectators below as if seeking for some person to whom he wished to give it; but he eventually delivered it to one of the officers of the gaol. The Chaplain then joined him again in offering up prayers for his salvation. Some persons in the crowd cried "Farewell Jobling!" and he replied "Farewell!" The Chaplain having retired, he commenced another prayer, in the midst of which, precisely at 20 minutes past 12, the drop fell and he was launched into eternity. He appeared to suffer much, and it was three minutes before he gave the last sign of departing life.

ADDRESS

OF THE

SPECIAL COMMITTEE

OF

THE COAL TRADE

TO

THE COAL OWNERS

OF THE

Counties of Northumberland and Durham,

ON THE SUBJECT OF THE

PITMEN'S STRIKE.

WM. HEATON, PRINTER, NEWCASTLE.

PITMEN'S STRIKE.

Address from the Special Committee of the Coal Trade to the Coal Owners of the Counties of Northumberland and Durham.

FOR the Causes of the present Strike your Committee refer to the Resolutions of the General Meeting of the Coal Trade of the 13th April last, to the Report of this Committee of the 27th of the same Month, and the Answer of the Committee dated the 13th instant, to the Allegations in the Speech of Mr T. S. Duncombe, in the House of Commons on the 4th instant: only here begging to recapitulate, that it has been proved by actual and incontrovertible Returns; That the Wages during the past year, and which the Coal Owners have offered to continue for the current year, are sufficient to enable the hewers on the average to earn 3s. 8d. in a working day of eight hours, free and clear of all deductions; in addition to which they have fire coal provided for them, and in almost every instance, their houses and gardens rent free; and, to each able bodied young man employed in putting, or two boys acting in the same capacity, the sum of 3s. 6d. per day of twelve hours, and others in proportion.

Notwithstanding the foregoing rates of wages, unequalled for similar labour in the kingdom, and the ruinous depression of the Coal trade, the workmen have struck to obtain fully 28 per cent. average advance upon these prices, together with such other requirements, as would place in a great degree the Collieries beyond the control of the masters. To accede to these demands would occasion the immediate abandonment of many Collieries, or lead to such enhancement in the price, as materially to curtail the export of Coal from these Counties. Under these circumstances the Coal Owners have resolved to oppose the most determined resistance to the unreasonable demands of their late workmen, and the Committee have the satisfaction to congratulate the Trade on the perfect unanimity of their Representatives.

The "Strike" having now continued, upwards of twelve weeks, without any certainty of an early termination, the Special Committee feel called upon to bring the existing state of affairs under the particular notice of the Trade.

The Committee have to express their regret, that the humane forbearance of the Coal Owners in permitting the general body of their late workmen to continue for so long a period, in the occupation of the colliery houses has not been at all appreciated by the latter; but on the contrary regarded with perverseness and thanklessness, and as a matter of right, rather than one of favour; and it is too manifest, that by actual assaults, turbulence and intimidation, endeavours have been constantly, and, in many instances, successfully made, by the parties thus suffered to remain in possession of the property of the Owners, to prevent the employment of other workmen willing to engage on the Collieries.

The Coal Owners, and indeed the inhabitants of these districts cannot be too grateful to the Lord Lieutenants, Magistracy, and other parties entrusted with the administration of the law, for the very judicious and prompt manner in which their duties have been respectively and efficiently performed. That the general peace has not been maintained without most persevering attention, is proved, by the very great number of persons who have been committed or held to bail since the commencement of the Strike.

The Committee fully appreciate the great and effective exertions which have been made for the bringing the Collieries into active operation. Already are 3639 men employed in hewing coals, of whom 766 have left the pitmen's union, and the produce of their labour is 5117 chaldrons per day, equivalent to about 3,729,000 tons per annum, and exceeding by 1,269,546 tons, the entire quantity imported into London from this district in the year 1843. The number of workmen resorting to the pits, and the consequent produce, are steadily augmenting, as proved by the weekly returns, and the Committee recommend that liberal encouragement be afforded to new workmen not previously employed as coal miners; and that they be assured of permanent employment.

The Committee would observe that the duration of the present Strike, is perhaps, one of the strongest proofs that can be adduced of the former actual comforts enjoyed, and property and credit possessed by the Colliers of these counties, and which have enabled them to subsist for 12 weeks in idleness, without, it is believed, material privation to themselves or families.—In truth the Colliers of Northumberland and Durham have never felt the vicissitudes in the rate of their earnings, that have been experienced in the manufacturing counties; as, when prices have been greatly depressed, the Coal owners have been the principal sufferers.

In conclusion, the Committee have to express their hope, rather, than their expectation, that the workmen may be induced to see the folly of their proceedings, and in the hopelessness of success, perceive the inevitable ruin in which they are involving themselves and families.

Great forbearance has hitherto been exercised in bringing into these districts, workmen from distant places, on account of the misery which such a proceeding must necessarily entail upon the misguided pitmen; it being obvious, that great numbers of them must in that case be left without employment, and themselves and their families consequently reduced to a state of destitution. The time however has at length arrived when this system of forbearance can no longer be adhered to. The trade must now have recourse to the extreme measure of obtaining a supply of workmen from other parts of the United Kingdom. The adoption of this measure involves the necessity of providing houses for the workmen to be so brought into these counties, and the consequent ejection of those who are now in possession; and who were only placed there upon condition that they should occupy them in their character of workmen, and consequently quit them, when they should cease to perform their duty in that capacity.

Coal Trade Office, Newcastle upon Tyne,
29*th June*, 1844.

Observations by the Committee of the Coal-Trade on the Discussion respecting the demands of their late Workmen, introduced during the Debate on the Motion to Repeal the Export Duty on Coals.

THE remarks of the Honorable Member for Finsbury on the evening of the 4th instant, when he took occasion to introduce into Parliament the subject of the Pitmen's Strike, have for the most part, been answered by anticipation in the Report of this Committee, published so long ago as the 27th April. But there are some of the Honorable Gentleman's observations which the Committee cannot permit to pass unnoticed nor uncontradicted, on account of the place in which they were made, the wide circulation they will obtain through the medium of the public press, and, the Committee would have added, the unfair spirit in which they were uttered, but for the conviction entertained by them, that the Honorable Member has been misled by a want of proper and impartial information on the subject brought by him before the House of Commons. In commenting upon the Honorable Gentleman's statements, the Committee quote from his Speech as reported in the Times Newspaper, and for the sake of clearness they have arranged their observations side by side with his own.

Observations of the Honorable Member for Finsbury.	*Answer of the Committee.*
"The Coal Owners are unwilling to go into the causes "which occasioned this "Strike."	In point of fact the Coal Owners have not any such "unwillingness." As regards the causes of the Strike, they are, it is conceived, the same with those which have occasioned Strikes in other parts of the kingdom, namely, to increase the wages of the workmen, and, more particularly in the present case, to abrogate the control of the masters over their own property.

"It was the Masters who "had Struck, and not the "Workpeople."

It is difficult for the Committee to understand the meaning of this statement. If it implies that the Coal Owners have forced a Strike by offering lower wages than were paid during the last year, this is contrary to the fact: for, though the state of the Trade would have justified a reduction, yet no such abatement has been made; the same prices for work having been proposed to the Pitmen as were paid them under their previous engagement: that is to say, sufficient prices to enable the hewers to earn 3s. 8d. per day of 8 hours working, free and clear of all deductions. The desire of the Coal Owners to carry on their works is shewn by the strenuous efforts they are making to supply the markets, by employing such hands as can be mustered. Already 1975 men are at work, and the number is daily increasing.

"There was no question of "Wages involved. It was "a question of the personal "safety of the men. A sys- "of Bonds too had been in- "troduced which had been "previously unknown."

The Committee experience great satisfaction in learning that the question is not one of wages, at the same time they cannot understand why, if no advance in wages is wanted, so great a one has been asked, as amounts, on the average, to at least 28 per cent. on the last year's prices, and in particular cases, to so much, that the collieries where it is demanded must altogether cease working from inability to grant it. Even the Pitmen themselves, who do uot seem to know very well what they have asked,make it appear in a published document that a considerable advance is required, though in reality their statement is very much short of the truth. As regards the safety of the men, the Committee are well aware, that in no part of Great Britain are Coal Mines conducted on superior, or even equally skilful principles, as compared with those of Northumberland and Durham; and in fact, more lives have been lost, not merely in a single storm at sea, but in a single shipwreck, than have been sacrificed in the entire mines of this district during the last fourteen years. Lest there should be any mistake on this point, which has been so much dwelt upon, the Committee have it in their power to state, from documents published by the pitmen themselves, that the annual average loss of life from accidents in the mines, has been no more than $1\frac{1}{2}$ per 1000, per annum, during the period in question. It is difficult to select an occupation in which fewer casualities occur: and it ought to be remembered in reference to accidents of a minor character, that scarcely any other class of labouring men have the privileges of Smart Money, Medical Attendancce, House, and Fire, which are possessed by Pitmen during the time they are suffering from misfortunes, which as frequently happen from their own want of precaution, as from any other cause.

The new system of bonds alluded to by the Honorable Gentleman, has been forced upon the Coalowners by the treatment they have experienced from their workmen during 11 months out of 12 of the last term of hiring. So early as May, 1843, the hewers began to restrict their labour, contrary to the letter and spirit of the Agreements, which provide that a workman "shall perform a full and fair day's work, according to each man's ability, such day's work not to exceed 8 hours." So far from this reasonable and moderate requisition being complied with, the Pitmen restricted themselves to an amount of work which on the average of the trade could be performed by a diligent workman in 5 or at the utmost 6 hours in the day, the object being, to check the supply, and to take advantage of the consequent rise in price, in order to enforce their demands. While this scheme proceeded, an attorney was engaged by the Pitmen, who made it his business to raise actions & commence chancery suits upon the yearly Bond, and to conduct the affairs of the workman in such a manner as plainly to evince, that the Coal owners could no longer submit to an instrument, which while it was binding upon them, was as events had fully proved, of no effect as regarded their workmen. It was determined therefore, for these and for other reasons which the Committee have fully explained in their report to engage the latter in a manner similar to that in which labourers and mechanics are hired in manufactories, and it may be said, in the mining districts of the kingdom generally; for the Committee are not aware that Coal hewers are hired for a service of 12 months in any other part of Great Britain: and, by consequence in none of the latter districts are the owners harassed by lawyers specially employed for the purpose of annoying them. The superiority in the condition of the Coal Miners of Northumberland and Durham has been heretofore most strongly marked. They have had better wages and more comfortable dwellings than other labourers of the same class elsewhere. The Coalowners hope and believe that this distinction in favour of their workmen will continue; but, should it be otherwise they appeal to the explanation which has been given as to whether they or the Pitmen will be to blame for such a result.

"The workmen declared "that they are willing to "submit all the disputed "points to a fair arbitration. "Would the masters meet "the proposal? If not, "could it be doubted they "were in the wrong?"

Assuming what the Honorable Member for Finsbury does not however seem willing to grant, that the question at issue is mainly one of wages, the Committee do not consider it necessary to answer the rapid succession of questions thus put by the Honorable Gentleman. They may however remark, that even supposing the principle to be admitted, it is absurd to think of carrying it out practically, by endeavouring to arbitrate on the affairs of more than 120 Collieries, employing upwards of 30,000 workmen. Not only would it be requisite to have as many arbitrations as there are Collieries, but with respect to every Colliery as many questions would have to be adjusted as there are different classes of workmen. The suggestion must have proceeded on the supposition, that the strike depended on some question common to the whole Trade, and is clearly inapplicable to the existing state of things involving so wide a range of local differences and character.

"But what were the other "grounds of conflict? One "was that the coal was "measured instead of being "weighed. The workmen "said that this arrangement "was unfair—that they had "a right to have their work "weighed, and they deman-

It is remarkable that the Honorable Gentleman does not know that the system of weight which he recommends so emphatically, in preference to that of measure, is precisely that which is being practised, and has been for a long time in use "ded that this arrangement "should be enforced. Why, "was there any thing so "very wrong in this? It "was only a year or two ago "that the system of measu-"ring coal in London was "altered at the instigation "of the Coal Owners them-"selves, simply because as "they said, and truly said "the measurement plan was "unfair to all parties. If "the Coal Owners then in-"sisted upon selling their "coals by weight, what rea-"son was there why they "should not remunerate "their labourers by estima-"ting the work done by a "similar test.?"

at the majority of Collieries in the Trade, and which, at its first introduction, was reluctantly agreed to by the Pitmen themselves. The Committee see no objection whatever to the plan of weight being generally adopted, especially if that of measure is considered to be " unfair to *all* parties," in which latter case they confess their inability to perceive how its continuance can be favorable to the Coal Owners. The Committee while on this subject would beg to remind the Honorable Gentleman, that the Act of Parliament substituting weight for measure in the sale of Coals, was passed not a year or two ago, but nearly 13 years ago, namely in October 1831.

"All they asked was, that "inspectors should be ap-"pointed to see that the "mines were made safe, and "that the subject of fines "should be properly and "equitably regulated. Why, "how was justice dealt out "under the present system? "Sometimes a man might "employ himself a whole "fortnight, and yet in con-"sequence of the operation

This statement is not incorrect, provided the workmen choose, as they have done for particular purposes, to inflict those penalties upon themselves, which it is their interest, as well as that of the Coal Owner, that they should avoid. Under any other circumstances the idea of a man finding himself in debt at the end of the fortnight is "of the fines, find himself in "debt at the end of that "time, instead of being in "receipt of a fair equivalent "for his labour."

nonsense, the real fact is, as has been shown long ago, that the fines amount to one halfpenny per day per man on the average throughout the Trade.

"A system, too, existed with "regard to payments, which "was most unjust to the "men: why were not the "payments made weekly? "At present the men were "only paid every fortnight, "and even then a week's pay "was kept back. (hear hear) "By this means, if a man "entered a work, for the "first three weeks he re-"ceived no wages at all, "and at the expiration of "that period only received "two week's pay."

The Committee are confident that if the Honorable Gentleman re-considers the subject, he will be aware, that the circumstance here mentioned, (and the extreme case is put) is of no importance to the Coal Owner, who has exactly the same amount of wages to pay whether they are settled immediately or after the lapse of some days. The only reason for having "running on days," as they are technically called, is to give time to the Overman, Hewer, and Owners to make out and examine the accounts, a matter not so simple as the Honorable Gentleman may suppose, when it is considered that the wages of it may be, some hundreds of people are to be settled, nearly all of whom are at work by the piece, and who are to be arranged and agreed with accordingly. The bare inspection of an Overman's bill, on a large Colliery, would convince the Honorable Member that it requires nearly a week's labor to draw it out properly and without error. That the contrary has been stated, is only a specimen of the vexatious and frivolous objections which have been raised against the Coal Owners in regard to the management of their own concerns: a line of proceeding which they are unanimously determined to tolerate no longer. Their workmen have been hitherto better paid than those of any similar class in Great Britain, and if they are resolved to sink themselves to the same level with others, the Coal Owners may regret, but cannot prevent the natural consequences of such conduct.

Coal Trade Office, Newcastle upon Tyne,
13th June, 1844.

WM. HEATON, PRINTER, NEWCASTLE.

THE QUESTION ANSWERED:

"WHAT DO THE PITMEN WANT?"

BY

WILLIAM MITCHELL,

PITMAN, OUSTON COLLIERY.

ALSO,

A LETTER TO THE COAL-OWNERS

OF NORTHUMBERLAND AND DURHAM.

BISHOPWEARMOUTH:
JAMES WILLIAMS, BRIDGE STREET.

LONDON: E. WILSON, BISHOPSGATE STREET; HETHERINGTON, HOLYWELL STREET, STRAND. MANCHESTER: HEYWOOD, OLDHAM STREET. LEEDS: HOBSON. NEWCASTLE: HORN, MARKET STREET; FRANCE AND CO., BUTCHER-BANK. SOUTH SHIELDS; M'COLL, KING STREET, AND ALL OTHER BOOKSELLERS.

1844.

[SIXTH THOUSAND.—FOURTH EDITION.]

"WHAT DO THE PITMEN WANT?"

The deep and general anxiety now felt in reference to this question, is at once a proof, that the pitmen's cessation from labour has already seriously affected the interests of other classes, and yet, that until now, these classes have not cared to know how that toiling mass have lived, by the product of whose labour the steam-engine plies its giant powers—the manufactures of England greatly owe their origin and importance, and all enjoy the comforts of an English fireside.

Such occurrences as strikes, if attended with inconvenience and injury, nevertheless seem occasionally necessary, to force attention to the condition and claims of the neglected classes of society. The pitmen's strike, however it may now terminate, will ultimately lead to an important amelioration of their condition. In undertaking to state the wants and grievances of his fellow-workmen—the pitmen of Northumberland and Durham—the writer does so with confidence, founded on a thorough knowledge of their condition and feelings, for, although he has been more accustomed to wield the pick than the pen, yet he hopes to be able to make their claims appear entitled to an attentive consideration.

That it is important that the case of the pitmen should be clearly stated and fully understood, will be evident from various facts.

There is a capital, it has been estimated, of upwards of fifteen millions invested in the coal-mines of Northumberland and Durham; not less than 25,000 workmen are required for the production of the coal. Except a very small portion, the whole of the shipping of the Tyne, Wear, and Tees, is employed in the coal-trade. The value of the shipping property thus engaged, cannot be less than £3,000,000, giving employment to vast numbers of seamen, and indirectly contributing to the support of thousands of others, butchers, bakers, shipwrights, smiths, sail-makers, ropemakers, &c.; in fact, there is not a trade nor profession in this district, that is not almost entirely dependent upon the working and prosperity of our coal-mines. The manufacturers of England never could have acquired their paramount ascendancy—the commercial greatness of Britain would have been unknown but for its mineral treasures, and of all its minerals, coal is by far the most important. The coal-mines have produced more wealth than all the gold and silver mines in the world. The total value of coal produced, must be several millions annually. I will now describe our occupation, in order that our peculiar grievances may be better understood.

Far from the light of day, we labour at the bottom of a mine, which varies from 300 to 1600 feet from the surface of the earth. There we toil in an atmosphere always vitiated, and sometimes surcharged with poisonous and explosive gases. These are principally of two kinds—"choke-damp," or "stithe," as it is called, is carbonic acid gas, and the other is "fire-damp," or carburetted hydrogen. Choke-damp is almost always present in the workings, and the inhalation of it is the fruitful source of asthma and other diseases, by which the life of the miner is shortened ten or fifteen years of the term of existence he would otherwise enjoy. Sometimes this choke-damp is so powerful as to produce instant death.

The loss of life which has occurred from explosions is terrible to record. From the accounts which have been kept, though these are very imperfect, and probably the loss has been much greater, it appears that the loss of life in the Durham and Northumberland mines, has been as follows:—

From 1803 to 1820,		
From Explosions,	501	
Inundated by Water,	75	
Choke-damp,	9	
Boiler-bursting,	18	
Other Causes,	22	
Total,	—	625
From 1821 to 1830,		
From Explosions,	341	
Falling of Stones, Choke-damp, &c.,	29	
Total,	—	370
From 1831 to 1843,		
Explosions,	391	
Other Causes,	60	
Total,	—	451
Total killed from 1803 to 1843,		1446

How many a home was desolated by the fearful sacrifice of life here recorded? It may too truly be said, that in such occurences it is the bereaved living who suffer; and what agony they endure, those only can realize who have experienced similar calamities.

It is due, however, to the coal-owners, to state, that with a spirit of humanity and justice, which reflects the greatest credit upon them, they have generally provided the widows, whose husbands may have been killed in their collieries, with houses and firing free, and made them a weekly allowance, as long as they remained unmarried. On nearly all collieries, the widows, if they receive no pension, live rent free. Yet, it will be apparent, when I describe the mode of working the coal-mines, that much might, and ought to be done to prevent the waste of human life, which has hitherto prevailed. I believe that with more competent and humane viewers, which the owners would have, by paying more attention themselves to the management of their collieries, and by a timely regard to their own interest and the claims of humanity, this annual sacrifice of their fellow-creatures' lives might be almost entirely prevented. The *Economist* newspaper, No. 34, in an able and interesting article, on the colliers' case, observes:

"There is more connexion between the present disturbances amongst the colliers and their physical discomfort, than may, at first sight, be thought. The soul and body are knit together by chords which never cease to vibrate; and, as a matter of business, a question of profit and loss, at the year's end, a matter affecting *their own* comfort, from day to day, we put it to these coal-owners, whether there is not something just now imperatively required at their hands, to soothe the feelings and soften somewhat the harsher features in the condition of these working men? Such a claim is made upon them, and we believe it is not made unjustly."

In endeavouring to describe, as clearly as I can, the mode in which the mines are worked, I invite the particular attention of those readers who may not be familiar with the subject, because it is only by understanding this part that they can appreciate many of the more important grievances of which we complain.

The preliminary process is to sink a *shaft*, which is done to the bottom of the seam intended to be wrought. Sometimes, but not generally, there are two shafts sunk. When this is the case, the one is called an "up-cast," the other a "down-cast shaft." The object of making two, is to effect a due supply of atmospheric air to the workmen, and the proper ventilation of the mine. The atmospheric air rushes down the down-cast, and the foul air escapes by the up-cast.* When there is but one shaft, the same object is accomplished, though imperfectly, by dividing the shaft into two parts, by a partition of wood, extending from the top to

* To secure a constantly descending current of atmospheric air, a furnace fire is generally made at the bottom of the up-cast shaft, which, by rarefying, or lessening the weight of the air, causes the heavier air above to descend the down-cast shaft; whence, by various contrivances, it is transmitted through the works. At Monkwearmouth colliery the heat of the mine is almost sufficient for the purpose.

the bottom, and called the "brattice-work." Commencing at the bottom of the shaft, the hewer proceeds to "drive," or cut, "headways," as they are called. This is usually done in a direction from north to south, or the reverse. These headways are driven to the extent of from thirty to forty yards in length, and from five to six feet in breadth. When driven that distance, the drivings, or cuttings, are then made in a direction from east to west, or *vice versa.* These drivings are called "stentings," "narrow-boards," and "wide-boards." Stentings are narrow cuttings, from four to five feet wide, made to effect a communication between one headway and another, for the purpose of ventilating the workings. A stenting is made every thirty or fifty yards, which the headway may be driven. The headways are, of course, extended as required, as far as the boundaries of the coal intended to be wrought. All headways are driven parallel to each other. Stentings, narrow-boards, and wide-boards, also run parallel to each other. The stentings being opened for the purpose of ventilating the workings; when a second stenting is opened, it is usual to close the first, otherwise the air, instead of passing on, as required, to the extremity of the works, would rush from the headway it entered, through the first stenting it reached, into the other headways, and thence return to the up-cast shaft, leaving the mine without a supply of air. If, however, the first stenting is not built up, when a second is opened, a door, called a "trap-door," is placed in it which is kept close by the pressure of the air against it. A boy, called a "trapper-boy," is placed to attend each of these doors,—to open it when a workman requires to come through such passage, and to close it instantly he has passed. On the trapper-boy's attention to this duty depends the safety of the mine and the lives of all in it;—for, if the door be neglected to be shut, of course the same consequence takes place as I have just pointed out, with the open stenting,—the atmospheric air is *not* transmitted, the foul air, therefore, instantly accumulates, and either suffocates the workmen by choke-damp, or involves the fearful calamity of an explosion. "Fly-doors" are frequently substituted for trap-doors. The fly-door is a door which closes, or *should* close, of itself. It has no trapper-boy. His services are dispensed with, to effect a paltry saving of tenpence per day, though this is done at the risk of the lives of all in the mine; for, if the "fly" does not *fly-too*, as it should do, choking, or exploding, must take place to a greater or less extent. Such doors are always objectionable, and ought never to be introduced. They are very liable, from various causes, to get out of square, and when so, will not fit close, by which the good air escapes, and the bad accumulates. A "narrow board" is also an excavation made from any headway, and is about six feet in breadth, and sufficiently high to admit a horse to travel through: being used for a passage, through which to convey the coals to the shaft, it has a railway laid in it, and such boards are therefore made as often as required, for that purpose. A "wide board" is the scene of the hewer's labour, and runs, like the former, from headway to headway. It is usually about twelve feet in breadth, but the height is limited by the thickness of the seam of coal, which the hewer there excavates. The seams vary in height from two-and-a-half feet to six feet, and in the quality of the coal of the respective seams, which are distinguished by different names, there is also a great difference. All are more or less mixed with foul coal, stone, or splint. One or other of these is usually found at the top, the bottom, or the middle of the seam. Foul coal is a slaty substance: splint coal is a dull-coloured common coal, which turns to white ashes, used chiefly for burning lime, or for iron-furnaces, or where great heat is required. The stones are generally of a dark colour, not easily distinguishable from the coal. The thinner seams are usually the most foul, and in these the hewer has to work in the most awkward and painful postures, lying on his side for hours together, with no better light than the dim one derived from a small candle, of which there are thirty or forty in the pound, or the equally inferior light of the "Davy," or safety-lamp. The temperature of the place in which he works, is but too well calculated to add to the severity of his labour. At Monkwearmouth colliery, while the mean temperature at the top of the bank is 47°, the temperature of the mine will be found from 75° to 90°.* It will therefore be apparent, that our labour, as hewers, is as exhausting to the system as can well be imagined. Now, to understand more clearly the injustice of some of the fines, it is most important to remember, what I have stated about the mixture of foul substances in the seams, and the fact, that the thinner seams, the most difficult to work, are also generally most foul. The coals, as wrought by the hewer, are conveyed in tubs, or large baskets, on a rolley, or small carriage, by the "putters," (boys or young men) to a central place, called a "crane," or flat whence they are drawn by horses to the bottom of the shaft. The tubs have hitherto been made to contain about twenty-two pecks, but latterly, in some of the collieries, larger corves, to contain about thirty-five pecks, have been introduced. This is a

* For a description of this mine and the mines of Northumberland and Durham generally, see *Chambers' Information for the People*, No. 97.

serious evil, for, from the weight of such corves when filled, the boys are unable to "put" them, without assistance, and the hewer has, without compensation, to quit his occupation to give the poor over-tasked putter-boy a "start." But the principal objection to these large corves, is, that they greatly impede the ventilation of the mine. In passing through the air-courses, they occupy the space, and leave none for the transmission of a due supply of air.

It may be as well to state here, that for the purpose of more effectually ventilating the wide-boards, where the hewers work, partitions of thin wood, called "brattices," are put up these boards. These brattices, by narrowing the current, increase the velocity of the air, and secure the purpose intended; but some viewers, impelled by blind selfishness, which oft defeats its own object, either leave the boards altogether without brattices, or by an insufficient supply of them, incur the risk of explosions, and endanger the lives of the men. At Sacriston colliery, until lately, no brattices were used, though the exposure of this neglect has since led to considerable improvement.

There are other sources of danger which I must briefly notice, —these are the roof or stones falling, and inundations. While engaged in our occupation, not unfrequently a stone, or a portion of the roof may fall, and either seriously injure us, or terminate our existence. Inundations have sometimes caused a terrible loss of life. That which occured at Heaton Main, May 3rd, 1815, deserves special notice, not merely on account of its awful nature, but also because we believe it to have been an event which, but for the *pride of science*, and contempt for the workmen's practical knowledge, would never have happened.

Heaton Main colliery, at the period in question, was under the management of the celebrated late Mr. Buddle, a gentleman, of whom it is a melancholy fact to record, that under his viewership more men lost their lives than under all the other viewers in this district. Not far from Heaton Main, was an old pit, called Jesmond colliery. This had been worked out, except the pillars, or blocks of coal, to support the roof, which are generally left till the last. The workings of Heaton colliery adjoined a former colliery of that name, connected with Jesmond pit. Mr. Buddle wished to work from the former into the latter, for the purpose of getting the coal-pillars that had been left in it. The communication between the two collieries was intercepted by a "dyke," or "trouble," as it is termed. This is a barrier of stone, or cinder coal, generally a few yards broad, but of great depth. Where they occur they alter the level of the coal seams. Mr. Buddle gave directions to cut through this dyke. In doing so, it was necessary to ascend from the level of the Heaton works. Many of the older workmen expressed their opinion, that it was a dangerous proceeding, that they believed the old works were full of water; but Mr. B., relying upon his scientific knowledge, which told him what *should be*, and having his plans of the pit workings before him, as his guide, paid little attention to these opinions. Disputes were frequent about the matter, but the cutting proceeded. The workmen who were engaged in this labour, observing the water drop rather heavily, were anxious to have the dyke bored, before proceeding further. After being bored, the hole could have been plugged up, if required. Mr. B., however, was imperative, he knew, from calculations, when it would be time to bore. At length, one morning, two of the men who were employed at the work, became so seriously alarmed, as to resolve to give it up. The under-viewer was with them, but he thought they might still go on. The men resolved to act on their own responsibility,—they knew they incurred the risk of *imprisonment, according to the bond*, for quitting their employment,—they consulted together, and concluded, that as the danger was a matter of opinion, they were not warranted in alarming the other workmen in the colliery. Most of the latter were working at a higher level than the bottom of the mine, where another portion were engaged. The total number in the mine was seventy-seven. These, except the two to which I have alluded, were toiling away, little anticipating their terrible doom. But scarce had the two men reached the bank, when their worst fears were realized. The partially cut dyke burst, and a mighty mass of water rushed into the mine, drowning, in one instant—all? No, not *all! some* were reserved for a still more dreadful fate; but of all the inmates, —fathers, sons, brothers,—all perished! With more than lightning rapidity the intelligence spread through the colliery village, and in a few moments the pit-mouth—that yawning entrance to a huge sepulchre—was surrounded with the bereaved relatives. Oh! what pen can describe the anguish of the mothers, wives, and children, there assembled. There, in the deep mine, were engulphed all that they held dear. They were not permitted to enjoy the momentary consolation of a deceptive hope, for the removal of that mass of water would be the labour of many months. It was so. Nine months elapsed ere it was cleared, and the bottom of the mine could be reached. But all were not *drowned*. No! There were those who were working in a higher level: what became of them? They were *starved to death!* But about their fate, there was, from the first occurence of the calamity, a dispute between Mr. Buddle and some old and experienced pitmen, who had worked in these mines. They thought that the level at which these men had been working was above the height of the water; that, therefore, they were not drowned, nor were they, in their opinion, suffocated, as Mr. B. thought; for, knowing by personal observation, how the old works of the collieries in that neighbourhood were ramified through each other, they conjectured it was at least possible that they might have a sufficient supply of air, to enable them to exist until they could be reached by some of the shafts and works of these pits. Accordingly, Mr. Buddle was anxiously urged to make the attempt, or permit it to be done; but still too confident in his scientific knowledge, and relying upon his colliery plans, he not only had no hopes himself, but would scarce permit those who had, to make the efforts they desired to solve the anxious question. An attempt, however, was made, to reach the sufferers by decending another shaft, but by Mr. Buddle's interference, it was abandoned before fairley tried, and the fact respecting their fate, remained undetermined until the water was withdrawn, a period, as I have observed, of nine months. What then was revealed? The first sight, in the higher portion of the works, that met the eyes of the few who were permitted to descend, was the bodies of the dead, lying dry, the water never having reached them! There were but too many proofs strewn around to shew they had died of starvation! There lay the remains of two horses, the flesh of which had contributed to support the unhappy sufferers! The bark from the fir props, the candles, of which there is usually a good supply kept below, and every thing which could be used as food, had been consumed. Opening the deputies' store chests, there was found the bodies of some boys, who had probably perished early, and had been so consigned by their surviving elders to such tombs. Marks were observed on the walls with chalk, which had evidently been done to note the progress of the water falling, and excavations were found to have been made, by which the miserable victims had attempted to effect an entrance into the adjoining works. There can be little doubt but they had survived a considerable time, and it was thought from appearances, that one of the strongest—Ralph Witherington, had died but a short time previous. This melancholy narrative, I trust, will not be deemed foreign to the question, "What do the Pitmen want?" They want, among other things, to be protected, as far as the law and public opinion, holding the viewers responsible for the lives and property entrusted to their charge, can protect them against calamities such as that just described, or such sacrifices as that which occurred at Wallsend, in 1835, when one hundred and two human beings perished by an explosion, Mr. Buddle, in this case too, being the viewer. The Heaton case is a sad proof of the danger of scientific bigotry, and the folly of treating with contempt the reasoning of unlettered experience.

Having now fully described the nature of our occupations, my readers will be prepared to understand and appreciate the importance of those grievances of which we more particularly complain in our present dispute with our employers, while I trust that the dangers and hardships to which I have shewn we are subject, will enlist a feeling of sympathy in our favour, and induce, both from our employers and the public, a fair examination of our claims, and a tolerant feeling for errors or faults which may have been committed.

The public will understand, that the engagement between us and our employers, was usually made by a document, called a "bond," many of the provisions of which were unreasonable and oppressive. Some may ask why we agreed to them? The question is foolish and unnecessary. Many causes might be assigned for our compliance, but there is no evidence that we were, or could be contented with them. The dispute between the owners and workmen of Thornley colliery, by which the colliery has been stopped, and the men thrown idle for twenty-three weeks past, occurred from an attempt to enforce some penalties in the bond, which had not previously been enforced. And why? Because they were so grossly harsh, as to be unfit to be enforced. This, Mr. Heckles, the viewer admitted, though he subsequently denied it on his examination before the magistrates at Durham, where the case was heard on the 7th December. Yet, even then, he said, in giving his evidence, "since the bond was executed, it has not been strictly enforced." It will occur to any one to ask, why was an agreement made which was not enforced? The reason may be inferred from the fact, that when it was "accurately enforced," which Mr. Heckles says, was on the 20th Nov., the amount of fines levied for "laid-out" tubs, (that is, tubs containing a certain portion of foul-coal, stone, or splint, was as follows: On the 21st Nov., £6 12s. 6d., and the 22nd, £5 11s. 3d. Some of the men, on these days, being fined 11s., 10s. 6d., 6s. 6d., and 5s. each. but this did not last. It could not. The men, instead of earning wages, were earning *debts*. Now, why was this? It has been attempted to be shewn, that the men were careless, or that they did this wilfully; but the assertion that men would wilfully bring themselves into debt, after toiling hard, is too preposterous to be believed. It has also, to strengthen that ridiculous assertion, been stated that the men were not so before, but the reason is plain. Mr. Heckles says, the bond relative to these fines was not "strictly enforced." The effects of "accurately" enforcing it was as I have shewn. But the iniquitous character of the bond is fully proved by the following evidence given on the trial:—

Wm. Henderson,—"Has worked at Thornley colliery since April last. More coal has been set out lately. The men have complained about the weights. The scales have not been adjusted to his knowledge. Is of opinion no man can make a living if the bond be enforced and every quart of stone be laid out. When he worked in the five-quarter seam, there was black brass from 1½ to 4 inches thick, and 4 inches of grey splint on the coal, and then 8 inches of stone. In hewing, all this mixes with the coal. It is impossible to gather it all out in a reasonable time. Can't get the black brass out, it is so near the colour of coal, by the light only of the Davy-lamp. There is also bad air, which almost stifles them, that they dont know what they are about. There is also the ten-inch coal, as it is called, comes down upon them, but not so regular as splint, &c. There are props under it, but it gets broken still. Has worked elsewhere, but no other bond so hard as this. Knows the men have applied to Mr. Heckles about rectifying the steel-yards. Has done so himself. Does not know that they have since been rectified. On the 20th Nov., he was *fined 6s. for one tub*. Only 3¾d. was to have been paid for the working of tub. There were twenty-four quarts laid out, at 3d. per quart. He would rather go to prison than work again under that bond."

Geo. Naisbitt,—"I worked at the colliery formerly—three-quarters of a year before. I heard complaints about the weighing machine. Some men sent to Mr. Heckles on the 13th Nov. *The bond was not enforced the previous part of the year*. I dont think it possible for average men to send up tubs without one quart of stones. It is the feeling of the men generally, that they had better go to gaol than work for nothing. I know men being brought in in debt to the owners. They were honest men and average workers."

Jabez Wonders,—"Has worked at Thornley colliery for six years. The bond was read when he signed it. Works in five-quarter seam. Was fined 12s. for three days' work, and stood 3s. in debt. He threw down 5s. and told the overman to take pay, but he refused. This was on Wednesday night. No man could possibly get a living if the bond was enforced. Did not know he should be fined for each quart."

When we consider the nature of the seam where these men worked, and the mode in which their labour had to be performed, it will be evident that it was monstrous injustice to fine them 3d. for only one quart of stone, out of twenty-two pecks of coal, and if two quarts were in the tub, the man was in debt. Well might Mr. Heckles say, it was not "strictly enforced." Why then was such a clause in the bond? It served the purpose of deterring the men from seeking their rights, and was there to be enforced when necessary, against an obnoxious man. In this case, the evidence of Mr. Heckles proved that it was not until after there was a dispute about a weighing machine, that the clause in question was "strictly enforced." In most of the bonds there are clauses not meant to be enforced, except for the purposes I have stated. In illustration of the grievances complained of, I shall give a few extracts from the *Miners' Advocate.* There are many other cases, all illustrations of injustice too general—the whole of them are duly authenticated, and, I believe, unexaggerated statements of facts.

The men of Walker colliery complain—"if a laid-out corf contains 4 quarts of splint or stone, we are fined *sixpence*, but we receive the corf; for hewing and filling the same we have *twopence;* if less than the 4 quarts, we loss the corf only."—*No.* IV., *p.* 30.

West Hollywell Colliery.—"Sir,—We wish you to make known to the public, through the Miners' paper, that there is laid out tubs at this colliery; we work the tubs at 4½d. per tub, and when a tub is laid out we are fined *sixpence*, leaving us 1½d. in debt for hewing such tub of coals! They fine us for sending small coals to the bank, and yet they are selling them for 6s. the chaldron; and we have to pay 3d. per week for the privilege of burning the same coals which we are fined 6d per tub for!"

Blaydon Main colliery-men say—"there is one clause in our bond, that we shall pay 3d. per quart for splint, stone, or foul-coal; and if any tub contain 4 quarts—*five shillings!* We have to pay sometimes for one laid-out tub, 1s. We have a band 6 inches thick, that lies in the seam, and in some places from 4 inches to 2 feet of stone, which comes down amongst the coals, and makes it almost impossible to keep clear of either laid-out or set-out."—*No.* X. *paye* 78.

In the same page and number, there is the following:—"In 1841, for a laid-out tub we lost the price for hewing, but in 1842 and 1843, we had to pay 4d. per quart for splint, jet, stone, or foul-coal found in any tub. As an instance of the manner in which we are fined, we beg leave to bring before your notice the following: A man was fined for one tub 3s. 4d., for another 3s., another 5s., another 5s. 4d., and for another 16s., and in mercy or human feeling for the man, we cannot say which, he had returned to him 6s.! We have known other men fined in a similar. These are not uncommon, and you will see in the following description of the seam, and the way of working it, how we are used. The seam is a splint seam, and we have to corve ten inches of splint square out, and throw the corving away, therefore it is hardly possible to keep clear of the splint. Sometimes the jet comes down with the top, and breaks so small, that it is impossible to get it all out; yet, if one quart be found in any tub, we have to pay 4d., and we receive nothing for taking it out."—*Miners of South Moor Colliery*.

Page 79, the Miners of Marley Hill Colliery observe, "they will say nothing about the 9 months that are past, with regard to our fines, but we do consider we are too hardly dealt with, they are as follows, viz.:—For 2 quarts of stone, foul-coal, or brass, 3d., for 4 quarts, 6d. We do positively assert, that it is out of the power of any man to take all the brasses out with a small candle, 30 to the lb. The coal being of a tender nature there does not many tubs of round come to bank; but in some cases, when one has come, the coals have been broken, the brasses taken out, and the hewer, therefore, fined accordingly."

From West Moor Colliery, a Correspondent writes, page 78,—"Now, Sir, I have given to the public a specimen of the 'set-out,' and shall now proceed with the 'laid-out;' it is this,—notwithstanding the men have only the dim light of the Davy lamp, or at most the light of a small candle, yet, if they send up a tub with 2 quarts of stone, splint, or foul-coal, no payment is made to the man for the same. Now, Sir, you will see that they have the light of day to see these stones or refuse, and the poor slave in his dungeon has almost to grope in the dark, and yet he is robbed and plundered in this shameful manner."

With respect to "laid-out" tubs, that is, those deficient in measure or weight, we have much reason to complain. The agreement is, that each tub shall contain a certain number of pecks of coals, or a certain weight,—by measure it is from 20 to 25 pecks, or by weight from 6 to 7½ cwt. Formerly the value of our labour was ascertained by measure only; when this was the case, if the tubs were deficient half-a-peck, they were set-out, or forfeited. We got *nothing* for the other 20½ pecks! The tubs always being larger than the exact quantity to be filled in them, we having to guess the quantity, in order to be safe, generally filled more. No allowance was made for what might be over. The average was not taken as it ought; but finding this system a ruinous one for us, we insisted upon having our labour ascertained by weight, and paid for the average. We have succeeded in obtaining this at most collieries, though some yet practice the old system; yet of those which conceded to pay us according to weight, some defrauded us by false weighing machines. Instances of this kind I will give. We were required, if we disputed the size of the tubs, or accuracy of the weighing machine, to give, formerly, three days; but, latterly, the three days were enlarged into the undefined and undefinable period of a "reasonable and sufficient notice, before we could get them examined. The three days' notice was of course diligently used in adjusting the corves by various ingenious contrivances, to prepare them for the inspector. What security would the law, for examining tradesmen's weights and measures, give to the public, if the inspector had to give to each shopkeeper three days, or, what he, the shopkeeper, would call a "reasonable and sufficient notice?" The latter notice having to be interpreted by the viewers, they generally took care to have sufficient for their purpose. The following case from the *Miners' Advocate* will prove this:—

West Moor Colliery.—"At the commencement of this year, we were bound to send to bank, in each tub, 6 cwt. of coal, and if a man's tub came up with $5\frac{3}{4}$ cwt. in it, he got nothing for it, consequently, the poor man worked the $5\frac{3}{4}$ cwt. for nothing, and gave them to the master, or rather, the master took them from him. But, Sir, the case will seem more ridiculous when it is shewn in its true light, and here it is. The masters of the above colliery had their tubs made to carry 7 or $7\frac{1}{2}$ cwt., consequently the working man had to guess a $\frac{1}{4}$ cwt. wrong, away goes the whole tub of $5\frac{3}{4}$ cwt. of coal into the masters' pocket for nothing, while the poor servile slave, who has been toiling all day long in a dark dungeon, exposed to danger on every hand, and of every kind,—such as the stone or coal falling, fire and choke-damp, or being lost with an inundation of water; notwithstanding all this, when he comes up out of his prison, he has, perhaps, a ton of coals taken from him. I myself have known it to be the case many a time, and sometimes more than a ton, nay, as far as *two* tons in a day, by laid-out and set-out. It would seem almost incredible that masters would or could do such things; but, alas, these are facts which are experienced almost daily by the poor colliers."—*Page* 78

Fawdon Colliery.—"We commenced to work by weight. This weight consists of 120lb to the cwt., and is called the long cwt., which takes 3 pecks more to the tub; we then stopped working, tried our machine and found it to be 19lb unjust. We sued for justice but none could be got. The additional 3 pecks to the tub is equal to 9d. per score. There is also a reduction of 1s. 9d. in the pillars, and 9d. in the whole. Under the present mode of working, each man averages the loss of 4s. 3d. per week, or £10 13s. per year. * * * * * We have been trying our weighing machine, and have found it to be unjust again, for which we have received the sum of £12."

East Cramlington Colliery.—"And lastly, though most important, by taking an account of the laid-out, we find in the Ann Pit, from July the 11th to Dec. 13th, in which time the pit worked 107 days, the laid-out, in that time, was 6249 corves at 7 cwt. each, which will make 2343 tons at 1s. 1d. per ton, £126 18s. 3d. for 107 days, or take the average for the year of 234 days, £241 6s. 4d.* In the Engine Pit, from July the 25th to Dec. 13th, in which time the pit worked 102 days, the laid-out in that time, amounted to 4641 corves at 7½ cwt. each, which will make 1740 tons at 1s. ½d. per ton, which will make £90 12s. 6d. for 102 days, or £207 13s. 6d. in the year; we have also a number of set-out corves, (that is, corves not weighing above 6 cwt.) which is forfeited to the master, as they must contain 6¼ cwt. before the hewer can get pay for them; these we have not kept a proper account of, but we have a considerable quantity set-out. We have lost by laid-out corves £448 19s. 10d."—*Page* 63.

I think it will now be admitted, that if the above statements are true, and that they are so, from my own knowledge and experience, I have no doubt, then surely the miners have some grievances; this system of oppression has existed too long, it is a system for the continuance of which there is no justification.

It is not by giving a flat denial to these statements, that the viewers can hope to succeed in persuading the public that 20,000 men have conspired together to invent and publish them without foundation. There is not a case here given, but can be established before any tribunal. The pay-books of the collieries to which they refer will prove them to be strictly true. Nor will the public be induced to believe that the extraordinary system I have exposed, can be requisite to insure the proper working of the mines. That there is a necessity for some penalties, I am not going to question, but having, since I penned the foregoing observations on fines, had my attention directed to a "Report of the Special Committee" of the Coal-owners, just published, I think it right to notice some of the reasons there assigned for the retention of the present vicious system. The committee say "that the fines are no hardship to a careful and honest workman, but merely operate as a due security against negligence and fraud." Now, I ought to be pardoned if I called this statement a great untruth; that it has roused my blood, the committee, if they have any "practical information," might expect. Why! *where* is the man who ever descended a coal-mine to hew, who does not know the statement is untrue? No "*honest* workmen feels the fines a hardship!" Where are the honest uncomplaining miners! Are all rogues? But I am glad the committee have put that in print, that statement will shew how far they will attempt, by bold assertions, to set aside facts. The committee, however, have done themselves retributive justice, in a very curious fashion, for they proceed to shew that the fines, after all

* The writer probably means the actual amount of fines for the 234 days.

are no loss to the parties fined. If that be so, then what becomes of the "security" they afford against fraud? To do the committee justice, I will give the entire passage:—

"As regards the liability to fines for securing this object (the committee are unable to devise a more equitable one than the one now in practice, under which the *amount of penalties* is necessarily considered in fixing the *amount of wages* to be paid for a given quantity of work, it being certain that in cases where the *drawbacks* from the workmen's wages are *greater* than the *usual* average, a *corresponding increase* of wages must, and does take place, in order to *equalize* the position of one colliery with that of others."

The committee say that they do not recommend abolition, but according to "the amount of the penalties," make a "corresponding increase of wages." The same rate of wages is paid to all the workmen. Now, all the workmen are equally subject to the drawback, or they are not; if they are, then the wages being made to correspond with the drawbacks, they balance each other, and the regulation is equivalent to no penalty. If, on the other hand, the drawbacks do not fall equally upon all, then those upon whom they do not fall, gain in proportion to the amount of the penalties. The higher the penalties the better for them. The committee have certainly proved themselves precious guardians of the coal-owners. Suppose a colliery of 500 workmen, where the penalties are high,—if 400 of the workmen were honest, the penalties would not operate upon them, the compensating wages would be a clear gain to them, and a loss to the owners. The owners would get nothing from them in the shape of drawbacks, therefore, under such a system, the owners would lose in proportion to the number of honest workmen they had on the colliery!

The committee, however, admit that the fines have been "excessive at some places for a short period," but in these cases the men, they say, willfully incurred them. The committee state that the fines have not averaged more than 1d. per head per day—*only* £1 6s. per year. If I lost £100 in a town containing 24,000 inhabitants, it would be no consolation to me to be told that my loss was only a penny per head. I have said nothing yet of the reduction in our wages, and it is not necessary to dwell upon it, because the masters admit they have reduced them, but they plead necessity for it. The reduction has been gradually going on from year to year, since 1831. Either in the shape of reduced price per score, or by increased measure or weight, in one form or another, reduction has been the invariable rule. The pleas have been various. Sometimes provisions were low, therefore we should be paid less. The coal-duty, before it was repealed in 1834, was at that time the plea used; but when it was repealed, and the trade extended, we obtained no advance. In 1842, the income tax and the re-imposition of the coal-duty, were urged as the grounds of a great reduction, which took place at the binding of 1843. Now, we know we cannot always command, nor ought to expect the same wages. We do not expect our masters to pay us wages out of their capital; but how do they reconcile the fact of the variation in the wages paid to us—their continued reduction, with the uniformity of price obtained by them for their coals? Until lately, very lately, the price of coals were the same as it had been forty years ago. In Porter's progress of the nation, a statement is given of the price per ton, from 1801 to 1835, from which it appears, the price, during that long period did not vary more than 9d. per ton. Since 1835, I have no certain data, but the result of enquiries that I have made, is, that until 1842, the original price was maintained. The reduction since has not been great, certainly not what would justify the reduction made in our wages. Let a fair comparison be made between our condition and that of other working men, and it will be found, that while the severity of our labour, the unhealthiness and danger of our occupation, are equal to any, our remuneration is inferior to most. The masters have asserted, that an average man may earn 3s. 8d. per day. The owners, acting upon the opinion that it is conducive to their interests, determine to sell only a certain quantity of coals, and thus have the power to limit the demand for our labour: by keeping up a compact union for that purpose, they have effected their object, viz.: maintained a high and uniform price for their coals, and they *may*, too, have realized a greater aggregate profit than they would have done by relying upon the natural laws which regulate the profits on other productions, but it is quite clear, that however it may have fared with them, we *must* have suffered by the demand for our labour being arbitrarily limited. We are, therefore, in self-defence, compelled to unite to protect ourselves against a course of policy so ruinous to us. They say there are too many of us,—that there are thousands more than they want; but if that be true, how much of our excess is the result of their policy? It is "too bad," when they have done so much to produce that evil that it should be used as a means of further depreciating the reward for our labour, a result by which not the public, but the coalowners alone would gain. Many collieries, during the last year, have not worked more than eight or ten days per fortnight, and I am informed that it has been ascertained, by returns carefully collected, that the average earnings of hewers, during the last year, have not exceeded 13s. per week. But allowing that they have earned 15s., that is not sufficient compensation. But they have not informed the public how many days per fortnight they permit us to work, nor of the various deductions for materials and tools made from our earnings.

I have now placed before you all that is essential to enable you to understand "what do the pitmen want?" They want to get rid of, or mitigate, the various evils that I have pointed out. This they have not only a legal and moral right te seek, but they would be deserving of censure if they did not. Discontent with what is remediable, and a desire for improvement, are great and essential virtues. They stimulate enquiry into the causes of evil, lead to their discovery, and call forth the needful energy to remove them. A spirit of aimless and querulous discontent chastises itself, but a yearning for an improved condition of existence is the result of some, and the harbinger of further, moral elevation.

Have we erred as to the means by which to obtain what we want? I do not mean to claim exemption from error, but while admitting our liability to it, I will proceed to lay before you what we have done, and to what further means we look to obtain our objects. Our grievances are of two kinds—those which admit of removal by law, and those which can be removed only by an equitable arrangement with our employers.

Under the first head, are breaches of agreement, or frauds, committed upon us by false weights, measures, &c. For these the law provides a remedy and to avail ourselves of it we have had to employ professional assistance. We thought we could secure this more efficiently by uniting to engage one man to devote his time and talents to our service, than by the former practice of each colliery procuring such assistance as they required it,—hence Mr Roberts' appointment. Mr Roberts, we know, has rendered us important aid, but it is in his legal capacity alone that we avail ourselves of his assistance. For other purposes we have an Executive Council, composed of men of our own profession. We have our "Miners' Union," which embraces the vast majority of Northumberland and Durham, and extends throughout England, Scotland and Wales.

We look to legislation to enforce if necessary, the application of means to ensure the safety of our lives and remove some of the sources of disease to which we are exposed. The nature of these means will be learnt from the following extract from the "pitmen's petition," drawn up, I believe, by a committee of gentlemen, belonging to South Shields.

"That the cause of those fearful explosions, is invariably the want of sufficient ventilation, which permits the accumulation of inflammable gas, or fire-damp, from the coal, in such large masses, as accidentally sets fire to, and explodes with such tremendous force, as sometimes to blow men up a shaft, 200 yards deep, as if from a cannon mouth, shaking the solid structure of the earth, in the neighbourhood of the pit, as if with an earthquake.

"That the lives of your petitioners are not a day nor an hour secure from such deadly operations, and, that it is a horrible and fearful thing to die such a death, or live in daily expectation of it.

"That, in addition to destruction by these sudden calamities, insufficient ventilation produces a vitiated atmosphere, from the poisonous gases and dampness of the mines, in which, from ten to twelve hours a-day, your petitioners are confined, breathing it under a severity of labour seldom practised on the surface, which brings on suffering, emaciation, disease, and early death.

* * * * * * * * *

"That your petitioners are clearly convinced, that while mines are allowed to be worked, as at present, with only a single brattice-pit to each, as in the greatest number of instances in those districts, through which are supplied 100, 200, 300, or 400, and sometimes 500 acres of under-ground workings, extending in some cases to upwards of 60 or 70 miles of passages, that the lives of your petitioners will continue in daily imminent danger, from the incapacity of one shaft to supply a sufficient quantity of air. Your petitioners are further convinced, that brattice-shafts, or pits divided by wooden partitions, are very imperfect, dangerous, and ill-fitted for securing proper ventilation, as they waste the air at its source, by allowing an escape from the down-cast to the up-cast, through a partition of about seven inches thick, the temperature differing between them, from 50 deg. to 60 deg. That in accidents they get easily deranged or destroyed; and, as is universally the case where they exist, are used at the same time for drawing coals with corves or tubs, which obstruct by the amount of their areas, the admission and egress of air in their already too diminutive capacities.

"That the only mode of securing proper ventilation, whatever direct means may be employed for securing it, is by always sinking two shafts to the coal or winning; and in proportion as the under-ground, making additional shafts. And thus would the whole mine be ventilated, the coals more easily and healthfully worked, and your petitioners secured from the recurrence of those terrible accidents."

The petition then points out the necessity of viewers, and under-viewers, having a scientific and suitable education, and asks for the appointment of inspectors, with authority to enforce requisite regulations. With respect to that portion of our claims, to the settlement of which we look to our masters, I have only to add, that it is their duty to give them a fair consideration, and it would enhance their claims to respect, were they to hold a friendly conference with a deputation of the most intelligent and judicious of our body, whom we should appoint to meet them. It is inconsistent in them to say that they are willing, as individual masters, to meet the men of their respective collieries, while they are bound to make no agreement unless with the consent and approval of a committee of their body.

It will be a source of deep regret to me, if aught contained in these pages should have a tendency to retard an amicable and equitable settlement. I have written to expose a system, not to wound the feelings of persons. There are many of the owners who are not aware of its injustice, and I know there are just and good men amongst them, who desire to treat their workmen fairly. May they all learu to rely more upon motives and influences addressed to the higher nature of man, than upon fines and penalties, or appeals to his selfish feelings. While other portions of society have advanced, we have not remained stationary. We no longer occupy the outer margin of civilization. Our present cessation from labour is distinguished by union, strict peacefulness, and calm determination. On these, and the fairness of our claims, we rely, and without fear, await the issue.

TO THE COAL-OWNERS

OF NORTHUMBERLAND AND DURHAM.

GENTLEMEN,—Having, in my pamphlet entitled "The question answered what do the Pitmen want," endeavoured to present to the public, a clear and truthful statement of the condition, grievances, and claims of my brethren, I now take the liberty respectfully to invite your attention to what I trust will be acknowledged to be a fair examination of the obstacles impeding the settlement of the dispute, a review of the course taken by you, and the position now respectively occupied. In doing this my sole object is to effect the termination of a struggle, injurious to both, a struggle, I think prolonged mainly by false pride and folly, while just and honorable mutual concessions might at once end it. I write not on behalf of my brethren officially, the sentiments I put forth are the spontaneous dictate of my own mind. I have taken no counsel but my own sense of duty.

The first great obstacle that appears to exist, on your part, to an equitable and speedy settlement of the dispute, is the extreme hostility you entertain towards the MINERS UNION. You appear to view it as a formidable conspiracy to deprive you of your legitimate authority, and to extort from you, by coercion, unreasonable demands. Permit me to say, in plain terms, but with no disrespectful feelings, that your prejudice against the Union of your workmen, is most unjust, and that your treatment of their demands is neither distinguished by candour nor reason. You claim, and have exercised unmolested, the right to combine to protect your profits—if union be necessary for you, it is much more so for us. You are wealthy, and powerful by your wealth—we are poor, and weak through our poverty. You are few in number, and enjoy a virtual monopoly of the coal-trade; we are many, too many by thousands, we are told, and our property, labour, is a commodity which we painfully feel, though from no fault of ours, is redundant. It is hard enough for servants, when masters are few, but when the few masters by combination, virtually resolve themselves into one, and when to maintain their interest, they limit the quantity of their productions, attempting to force a large profit from a small trade, and by that limited trade create an unnatural excess of labour, *then* it becomes imperative on the owners of the latter to combine to defend themselves against the tendencies of the former combination. While, therefore, your union exists, ours must. We have more than your necessity for union, if its utility to us be questioned we plead your example. We act defensively—aid us to remove the necessity, by perfect freedom and justice, and we will gladly abandon our standing army. Your example sanctions, and the law of the land recognises our right to unite. It appears to me that those who are most hostile to our union are those whose conduct has done most to cause it. Rebellion is the wages of tyranny and I am sorry to have to state, that the conduct of your servants, but our masters, the viewers, has, with some honourable exceptions, been as mean and despotic as that of the petty princes of Germany. Having held a delegated, but yet an almost absolute despotic power they have, too generally, governed us in an arbitrary and tyrannical manner. Their irritating conduct has produced bitter discontent, and they, to justify themselves, calumniate us to you, and insist on the necessity of maintaining their unjust and arbitrary system of fines and penalties, which make a pitmens' bond the most disgraceful documentary engagement, that any class of working men are subject to. Generally speaking, you, like the absentee landlords of Ireland, know little of, and that little knowledge tends to produce little regard for, those from whose labour you derive your incomes. You may say this is idle declamation, that if we had any grounds of complaint of your servants, we should, each man for himself, appeal direct to you. We have done that, and many of my brethren have felt the consequences of it, for however it might share with the complainant at the time, he was sure to be a marked man, and generally, sooner or later, was discharged by the viewer of whom he complained, and when dismissed for such an offence, he found it was one which no viewer would pardon, the knowledge of which preceded him to every colliery where he applied for work, and the consequences, therefore, of which he could only avoid, by *changing his name*, and as far as possible concealing all clue to his identity. Many instances of this kind have occurred. It was such results that led to the formation of our Union in 1831, and it has been the helpless ness of individual resistance felt since 1832, when our former Union was bro ken up, that has once more led to the Union of all for the protection of each. For years previous to 1831, our condition had been rapidly deteriorating, and our treatment was growing more and more harsh. Numbers were left unbound every year, not so much because they were not required, as that they being compelled, through destitution, to seek relief from the poor-rates, the same masters who had refused them employment, might there assign them work on the roads at such a sum as would induce others to accept with thankfulness the reduced wages offered for working in the pits. While the men were thus treated, their sons, from 7 years of age and upwards, were kept toiling down the mine from 14 to 16 hours a day. It is no exaggeration to say that many scarcely saw the sun except on the Sabbath day. The strike of 1831 enabled us to modify that oppression. Yet at that period our demands were resisted with as much pertinacity as now, our Union was denounced as illegal and tyrannical and our leaders as demagogues. The strike terminated when the Marquis of Londonderry, judging for himself, and resolving not to be hoodwinked by others, broke from your union, conceded the principal portion of our claims, and thus compelled the remainder of your body to come to a similar agreement. But this concession was made with a reluctant spirit, the Union which had effected it was proscribed. Accordingly, in 1832, another struggle was forced on, the issue was for the time most unfortunate for us and was thought by the masters to be a great triumph for them. But was it *really* so? Was it not accomplished by bringing a mass of workmen, at a great expense, from other parts and superseding through their labour, to a considerable extent, the services of the regular pitmen. No sooner did the latter submit, than the viewers knowing that their skilled labour was more valuable, discharged most of the strangers, violating in many instances, the engagements made with them and leaving them to return to their former homes as they best could. The miners of Weardale, Yorkshire and Lancashire, know this too well, and it is the remembrance of it, that renders your present efforts to procure their services so fruitless. I have advanced sufficient to shew the origin, and to justify the existence of our Union, yet you say you will not recognise it. We do not ask you. Two local newspapers, in articles distinguished for talent, but bad temper and gross partiality have sought to befool you and the public, by systematically mixing up with the dispute between us matter which has nothing whatever to do with it. I will not permit myself to be dragged away from the question by the trickery of these unmanly assailants. The animus of at least one of them it is shrewdly guessed has its origin in the desire to crush a professional rival—that spleen at the non-participation in the Pitmen's law fund, is more conspicuous than any concern for your interest. Unfortunately you regard our legal adviser as our dictator. In this you are grievously mistaken. We understand our own grievances, and with reference to them we act on our own judgment. Because the name of an individual obnoxious to you, is affixed to our bond, you will not it appears consider it. Need I remind you that it is the things in the bond, we claim, we care not by whom it is drawn out, provided we are satisfied with its terms, and that these are expressed in clear language, and made mutually binding, as the law requires. We want nothing left to the caprice of individuals. No Thornley colliery clauses, unfit to be "accurately enforced." We have never hesitated to avow our readiness to make reasonable concessions when you are prepared to meet us in a similar spirit. You cannot, I think, maintain the perfect justice and propriety of your bond. The main points of difference between us are wages, fines and penalties. With respect to the first, we claim an increase not exceeding the amount of recent reductions. On some collieries the increase is the merest trifle, on others it is considerable, but this is because the latter have been paying much less than others, why then should the former make common cause with the latter. Let those who have collieries, that will pay for working, work them, but why should you refuse to concede what is just, because we have united to obtain it. Perhaps you think the leaders of the Union suggest unreasonable demands and infuse an improper spirit into the minds of the men. This is a great mistake, their influence has uniformly been exerted to produce a different result. It was natural that it should, being pitmen themselves, and neither as delegates nor lecturers receiving pay for their services they are interested in effecting a speedy settlement. They know that they are held responsible for the acts of the whole body. They have therefore the most powerful motives to enforce a peaceable demeanour and to terminate the dispute as soon as our reasonable claims are met. The spirit in which the strike has been conducted has commanded the respect and commendation of all classes. Statements have from time to time been published by your authority, professing to give a fair representation of the wages paid to us and of the loss you would sustain by giving the increase we ask. Though it may be unknown to some of you, yet it is nevertheless the fact, that many of these statements have been grossly unfair. I believe there is not a colliery on the Tyne, Wear, nor Tees, where the average amount of wages earned *and paid* has been 3s. 8d. per day or 22s. per week. We have learnt of many where the wages have been half that amount, and we here give a statement of the *highest amount* of wages earned by *any man* on the following collieries, and challenge any one to prove it false.

Names of Hewers.	Names of Collieries.	Gross earnings from April 6th, 1843, to and with April 5, 1844.			Deductions for powder candles and firing.			Pick Sharpening.		Picks made and repaired.		* Fines and forfeitures.			Gross amount of deductions.			Net income.			Weekly average.	
		£	s.	d.	£	s.	d.	s.	d.	s.	d.	£	s.	d.	£	s.	d.	£	s.	d	s.	d.
O. Detchin ……	Spital Tongues,	43	0	0	3	7	9	4	4	5	6	0	17	9	4	15	4	38	4	8	14	8½
R. Coulson ……	South Hetton,…	35	0	4	3	15	11	4	4	7	0	0	0	0	4	7	3	30	13	1	11	9½
Wm. Greenwell,	Kibblesworth,…	32	18	5½	2	8	0	4	4	6	6	0	12	1	3	10	11	29	7	6½	11	3½
Wm. Bulman,…	Coxlodge, ……	34	1	10½	0	0	0	0	0	0	0	0	0	0	4	19	8	29	2	2½	11	2¼
Wm. Knaggs,…	Urpeth, ……..	35	13	9	2	3	9	4	4	5	6	0	2	6	2	16	1	32	17	8	12	7¾
W. M'Millen …	Woodhouse Close	30	15	7	2	8	0	0	0	0	0	†3	12	6	6	0	6	24	15	1	9	6¼
E. Hall, ………	Walker, ………	39	14	6½	0	0	0	0	0	0	0	0	0	0	1	12	10¾	38	1	7¾	14	7¾
	South Moor, …	36	4	11	3	5	0	4	4	8	6	0	0	0	3	17	10	32	7	1	12	5¼
	Totals, ………	287	9	5½											32	0	5¾	255	8	11¾	12	3¼
General average, 12s. 3¼d.																						

* The amount of fines here stated is much less than what the men have really paid, but some men having kept no account of their fines and forfeitures I am unable to give them.

† House rent.

The foregoing table gives a true representation of wages actually received, and it will be observed, from it that we have *not* our firing free, that a deduction is made, nominally for leading, but really for the value of the coals used by us. In the cases where the charge for firing does not appear, the parties are unmarried men, and of course, the coals will be charged to the persons with whom they lodge. Why should this dispute be prolonged? Do you think you will induce the men to submit to the bond you offer? You never will. If you were to defeat and utterly crush the men what would you gain by it? The bitterness of feeling and the recklessness regarding your property and interest that would ensue would make your victory an unprofitable one. It is intimated, that you contemplate introducing a horde of *navies* and Irish labourers, into the pits, instead of us. What would you gain by that? If you could carry it out, you would make an immense pauper population which you would have to bear your share in supporting, and would not the natural tendency be to lead to crime, and acts of violence, which all good men would deprecate, and by which all would suffer? Calculate the cost of obtaining such men, the loss which must be sustained in training them, and the fact that you *must* pay them at least ordinary labouring wages, then compare the difference between that and what we claim, and you will, I believe, find the balance against the scheme. Let me assure you that this project will produce no panic amongst your workmen, they know that it will never answer; however I again express my hope that some one or more amongst your body will confer with us as men capable of reasoning and not insensible to justice. We believe you to be so. Meet the men on your respective collieries if you will, state to them what concessions you propose, or discuss the points in difference between you and them, but be not so absurd as to censure them if they should not decide at once while *you* have expressly declared your inability to do so unless by the consent of others. Hoping that ere long an honourable and happy settlement may be made.

I am, Gentlemen,

With the greatest respect,

Your humble servant,

WILLIAM MITCHELL.

May 23rd, 1844.

BISHOPWEARMOUTH: PRINTED BY WILLIAMS AND MORRISON.

British Labour Struggles:
Contemporary Pamphlets 1727-1850

An Arno Press/New York Times Collection

Labour Problems Before the Industrial Revolution. 1727-1745.

Labour Disputes in the Early Days of the Industrial Revolution. 1758-1780.

The Spread of Machinery. 1793-1806.

The Luddites. 1812-1839.

The Spitalfields Acts. 1818-1828.

Friendly Societies. 1798-1839.

Trade Unions Under the Combination Acts. 1799-1823.

Repeal of the Combination Acts. 1825.

Trade Unions in the Early 1830s. 1831-1837.

[Tufnell, Edward Carlton]
Character, Object and Effects of Trades' Unions; With Some Remarks on the Law Concerning Them. 1834.

Rebirth of the Trade Union Movement. 1838-1847.

Labour Disputes in the Mines. 1831-1844.

The Framework Knitters and Handloom Weavers; Their Attempts to Keep Up Wages. 1820-1845.

Robert Owen at New Lanark. 1824-1838.

Motherwell and Orbiston: The First Owenite Attempts at Cooperative Communities. 1822-1825.

Owenism and the Working Class. 1821-1834.

Cooperation and the Working Class: Theoretical Contributions. 1827-1834.

The Rational System. 1837-1841.

Cooperative Communities: Plans and Descriptions. 1825-1847.

The Factory Act of 1819. 1818-1819.

The Ten Hours Movement in 1831 and 1832. 1831-1832.

The Factory Act of 1833. 1833-1834.

Richard Oastler: King of Factory Children. 1835-1861.

The Battle for the Ten Hours Day Continues. 1837-1843.

The Factory Education Bill of 1843. 1843.

Prelude to Victory of the Ten Hours Movement. 1844.

Sunday Work. 1794-1856.

Demands for Early Closing Hours. 1843.

Conditions of Work and Living: The Reawakening of the English Conscience. 1838-1844.

Improving the Lot of the Chimney Sweeps. 1785-1840.

The Rising of the Agricultural Labourers. 1830-1831.

The Aftermath of the "Lost Labourers' Revolt". 1830-1831.